Jesus Doesn't Say Please

Jesus Doesn't Say Please

Robert Weyrick

WINEPRESS WP PUBLISHING

Printed in the United States of America.

Packaged by WinePress Publishing, PO Box 428, Enumclaw, WA 98022. The views expressed or implied in this work do not necessarily reflect those of WinePress Publishing. Ultimate design, content, and editorial accuracy of this work is the responsibility of the author(s).

ISBN 1-57921-363-4
Library of Congress Catalog Card Number: 2001086783

For my family and to my wife Denise and my sons Jesse and Jordan. Thank you for being my partners in life.

Special thanks to all our long term donors including: Arne and Jenny, Scott and Jane, Porter and Lois, Leon and Ann, Jaunita, Keith and Claudette, Duane and Deanna, The Meerdink Families, The Watson's, Dave and Stephanie, Richard and Rosalyn, Lyle and Carol, Jon and Sheryl

Special thanks to our supporting churches including: Shoreline Christian Church, Lopez Island Community, Maple Leaf Evangelical, Overlake, Eastside, Normandy, McKinley Park, Southlake Shore, Lake Sawyer, Pasco, Centralia, Florence, Oregon City Evangelical and West Seattle Womens Group.

In appreciation to my best friends and buddies who keep me honest and help me laugh: Bill, Phillip, Jon, J.B., Kevin, Ken, Whitney, Rich, Brad, Bredvik, and Sawyer.

And finally to the Network Board and Staff. Thank you for listening to my dreams for ministry and working together in the Kingdom. God is Good.

Contents

Foreword

Babies cry a lot. Whenever they need something they will let you know. A baby that wants something can be relentless. Warm milk in a bottle, a diaper change, or a distracting hug will usually solve the problem.

Eventually babies grow up to be people with responsibilities. Of course this only happens if someone nurtures and cares for them.

This book is my attempt to nurture and teach you about King Jesus. As you read this book I hope you will understand that I am not a baby sitter and this book is not a bottle of warm milk. I do hope this book will help you grow in your relationship with God. Everyone has a relationship with God. The status of that relationship depends on you. God has revealed His position and He wants to have a loving relationship with you.

Just like a baby eventually leaves the bottle and begins to eat real food, the new Christian needs to expand their diet of spiritual food to include meat in addition to milk.

This is not a self-help book. This is a help yourself book. My prayer is that you will take Jesus seriously and find the time to study your Bible. God's goal is to harvest goodness from your life. That harvest will cost you time and money. If you are unwilling to invest in your walk with King Jesus, you will remain a baby and be lost in immaturity and self-satisfaction. *'Jesus doesn't say Please'* follow me, He says follow me. If you are waiting for Him to get down on his knees and apologize to you for the hurts and harms of life, you might want to take an overnight bag. Jesus may not be who you think He is.

Part One

Jesus is the Hard Line of Division

Chapter One

Let's Kill Jesus

Who was Jesus? What kind of man was he? Was he a good teacher strolling with his disciples throughout the countryside, advocating a new philosophy? How about a latter-day Confucious or Buddha, spreading tidbits of wisdom and practicing socialized medicine? Or perhaps, a "feel-good" consensus builder, teaching us to love everyone and embrace unconditional tolerance?

These are questions that have been asked throughout the centuries, by both theologians, teachers, and the man on the street? In fact, if you described Jesus in any of the above ways, or similar such phrases to that man on the street you would get an affirming nod or far-away look of contemplation. More alarming, if you asked the average church-goer in the United States the same thing, you'd get the same response!

How about Jesus' advisaries? How did they respond to his character and his ministry? Were they a handful of trouble-makers or arrogant representatives of the 'establishment'? Maybe, just a group of stick-in-the-mud, conservative clergy, always quick with a disapproving look or contentious question. The euphamistic filter of time and watered-down Christianity has portrayed them as a few frustrated, jealous, religious leaders who managed to rile up a normally adoring crowd at just the right time during the Passover.

Scripture and history, however, tells quite a different story about Jesus, his ministry, and his enemies. The fact is, the ministry and message of Jesus were *not* well received. The crowds surrounding him were fickle and short-lived. Jesus was baptized by John the Baptist in the spring or summer of AD 27. By the spring of AD 29 he was very unpopular. His healings had caused divisions, His teaching had people confused, and His disciples did not understand His mission.

Early in each Gospel we read how the leaders of his day wanted to kill Jesus. There are several recorded events of near, and narrowly avoided, assassination attempts. Without a doubt there were many more incidents not recorded in the Gospel accounts. It would not be a stretch to assume that on some of those occasions that Jesus would retire with his disciples to "a lonely place", it was more than just an attempt at a spiritual retreat. *Our* culture views Jesus as a winner who was a great teacher. *His* culture viewed Him as a whiner who needed to be silenced. Specifically, the unspoken introductions would go something like this.

"Hi, I'm Jesus the teacher".
" Great to have you around," the leaders say "Oh and by the way . . . could we kill you later this afternoon".

The followers of Jesus enjoyed a very short honeymoon after Jesus left them in Jerusalem. Many cultures following the early days of the Church tried to silence the Message of Jesus. For instance, Christianity was an illegal cult for three hundred years. The early Christians in Rome met at night in the secret caves of the catacombs

Contrary to popular opinion, external opposition wasn't the only attempted impediment or characteristic of Jesus' mission and life. Jesus, himself, tried to minimize mass exposure to his ministry. He tried to *escape* the crowds , not attract them. Most of the crowds we find gathered around Jesus were there to get something from Jesus. They wanted to be healed or fed or freed from the oppression of the Roman Empire. To say that Jesus was fed up with the crowds would be an understatement. Jesus' goal was to be a suffering servant, *not* a successful celebrity.

Church growth proponents want us to believe that Jesus attracted a crowd so that he could have a big following and now, we need to model Jesus' ministry so that we, in turn, can bring big crowds to church. I am all in favor of church growth, but I am not sure we should use the pattern and nature of New Testament crowds as a Biblical basis to promote growth.

Nowhere in the Scripture do we find Jesus pleading with people to follow Him. In fact, the exact opposite is true. On several occasions in the New Testament record of the life of Jesus, we find him asking crowds to leave him alone. We find him seeking out time by himself or wanting time alone with his students. Jesus does not say "please follow me."

The best example of this approach to crowd management might be in the book of John, chapter six. Here, we find Jesus trying to be alone after the execution of his cousin, John the Baptist. The parallel passage in the book of Matthew, chapter 14 tells us about the circumstances surrounding the timing found in John. While Jesus is just trying to have some time alone, the relentless crowd follows him to be healed and get a free meal.

Why would the Messiah heal people and then tell them to keep quiet about it? Why would he leave crowds of followers behind so he could go and teach in other cities? The answer is that Jesus was not waiting to be accepted. Jesus was not hoping to be popular. Jesus was not looking to be published or trying to establish a successful ministry outreach. Jesus was waiting to die.

Throughout the Christian Age, people have questioned as to why Jesus waited until he was thirty years old to begin his ministry. Is there really any wonder? Jesus was not in a hurry to begin because he knew people would reject, hassle, and resoundly disagree with his message. The view of the first century political, economical, and social stage is not that much different from the world view today. How do you think the message of Jesus would be received today ? Do you think the ACLU would endorse him, could he run on the Republican or Democratic ticket. If you believe this, you do not really understand the message that Jesus brought to the world. His message has never been one of political compromise.

Would Wall Street recommend investment into the Jesus movement? His message has never been one of economic abundance. Would the Red Cross recruit Him as a volunteer to feed the worlds hungry and fix the worlds pain? His message has never been one of social management.

His Mission was to divide history. His message—closeness to Him comes by *dying* to self. Greatness comes through sacrificial love and service. He said " Do you think I came to grant peace on earth? I tell you no, but rather division (Luke

12:51)." From the manger to the cross Jesus made people decide who they would follow and *He never said please!*

People have also wondered why Jesus did not stick around longer on earth. Why did he die so young? He could have taught until he was sixty and then retired in the Mediterranean. Yeah right. I'll bet he just could not wait to be questioned by the authorities for *another* thirty years. I have often wondered why he stayed so long!

If you really want to get to know Jesus, get ready to have your entire thought process rearranged. Jesus never leaves people the way he finds them. Everyone is drastically changed by exposure to Him. The seeker or the skeptic will not leave an encounter with Jesus unchanged. Let me illustrate this point by relating a story:

My wife and I used to enjoy traveling, now we travel with our children. We still enjoy the journey, but it is a lot more work to travel with kids. In 1981, before we had our two boys, we grabbed our ten speed bikes and boarded a ferry to Victory B.C. from Seattle. We spent three wonderful days touring the city.

One day we rode out to the Canadian version of SeaWorld where some killer whales put on a fish eating show. From the time we entered the training facility there were continual announcements about where to stand during the show. Additionally, there was a color system that let you know how wet you might get when this whale, the size of a small condominium complex, jumped out of the water and then, came back down—If you where standing in the blue area you would be in no danger of getting wet. If you were in the yellow area you *might* get wet. If you were in the red area you would *definitely* get wet. They must have announced this at least ten times before the show started. Of course, the best view of the show was from the red colored area!

There was a group of older tourists who came in a little late and filled up the red area because it was so close and convenient. The warnings about being prepared to go swimming if you were in the red area continued for another few minutes and some spectators from the more "mature" group decided to head for higher ground. The more daring visitors from the retired tour group decided to stay in the red area.

My wife and I were perched on top of some dumpsters just above the forewarned red section when the baby whale made her entrance. This baby was only the size of a small mini-van. When she lifted up out of the water the people in the red section had a spectacular view and just got the lightest splash of salt water on their shoes when the baby landed. Then came big mama whale. She was large. She was fast. When she came out of the water a shadow fell over the red area. Then she came down like a blimp out of the sky. My wife and I watched as the first four rows of visitors were totally engulfed by a wave of sea water. Several older women were knocked off their feet. Purses and camera bags were filled with water. One man had his hat knocked off and was frantically trying to swim for it. It was one of the funniest scenes I have ever seen. From our dry perch we watched the entire crowd react with the same thought—"Didn't you hear the warning?"!!!

Jesus is just like this. He will warn you where not to stand and display by *His* example where He will be standing. Then, He will let you stand anywhere you want. When your life is over, don't try to complain to Jesus that you did not understand. He has warned you over and over again, not only in the Bible, but also through your personal experiences. People think that Jesus will have good manners and say "Please don't stand in the red punishment area."

Jesus does not say please. He warns you like a King would warn a servant, like a boss would warn an employee, like a Father would warn a child. He *might* say please, but he does not *have* to. He *might* be gentle, but don't count on it.

The nature of man has not changed since creation. Today's post modern man would reject Jesus and his message just as quickly as the Alexandrian infant Roman culture of his day. The clash of ancient cultures from Sumerian Ritualistic Cults to Egyptian Pyramid Tombs would crush the message of love and gentleness that Jesus preached. Cultures before Christ would have rejected him just as his own culture crucified him. Jesus is no stranger to rejection.

The point of concern for the skeptic, *or* the believer, should be the response that *Jesus* shows to such rejection. He promises retribution in spectacular fashion, as seen in several passages, specifically directed at those people who reject Him. The modern day Gospel of Tolerance or the regurgitated old "New Age" think tank will have problems with Jesus and the way he promises to deal with obstinance and rebellion. Jesus can command us to love others and tolerate the sin of the sinner *without* committing himself to be some gentle guru who will never judge others.

That is the advantage of being a Monotheistic Dictator. His will is the ultimate outcome, regardless of opposition or slander. Our picture of Jesus is skewed by historical attempts to remove the tenacity and authority of His leadership style. In our western culture we almost expect Jesus to be polite and respectful toward the way we behave. We have a western Jesus that would not dare to interrupt our indulgences. Our Jesus would not be to loud, to self centered, or to demanding. The only problem with this western Jesus is that the Jesus in the Bible was the center of attention, did get loud on occasion, and is, without a doubt, demanding as He commands the universe.

Can You Trust What Jesus Says?

God gives us the right to choose. The doctrine that man has a free will is presented throughout the Bible. In theological circles, there is an ongoing debate between the free will of man and the doctrine of predestination. Both are taught in the Bible. Calvinists tend to get the cart before the horse and teach predestination as the primary doctrine in the Bible. Clearly the horse that leads the cart is the free will of mankind. Without free will there can be no choice to submit our will to Christ. Jesus submitted his will on earth. The very presence of Jesus on earth was an act of submission. We are also asked to submit our will.

Jesus may have been a man of few words. We have no ancient record of his personality. Theologians have been engaged in higher criticism of the New Testament for thousands of years. Scholars have concluded that the synoptic gospels of Matthew, Mark, and Luke were written from a lost record of the sayings of Jesus they have labeled the Q document. This lost document was developed from the oral traditions circulated by the early followers of Christ. I remember the first time I read about Q. I was amazed that intelligent people would care about a document that they did not have. Since then I have studied the importance of the oral tradition or Kerygma message the Apostles and early believers talked about before anything was written down.

In all the records of what Jesus said we have no clear idea about his personality. Was he funny? Did he laugh and find humor in everyday situations? Maybe he was dry and serious. Maybe he was impatient with the small-minded people who surrounded Him. Are the words attributed to Jesus in the Bible the exact words Jesus said? Do we have an exact record of every word Jesus said? The words in the Bible attributed to Jesus are the inspired recollection of eye-witness testimony that was written, recorded, or investigated years after the actual event happened and the words were spoken. The inspiration to write down the words of Jesus in a permanent record was orchestrated by the Holy Spirit. The Holy Spirit has left us a record of a leader who did not plead with His followers. The writers of the New Testament tell us in several places that Jesus is in charge of life after death, and that the only way to enter life after death is to submit your will to the kingdom of Jesus. People can argue with Jesus until the stars lose their shine, but the empty cross will stare back as a testimony that Jesus is the only leader of any kingdom that was able to overcome death.

Eyewitness accounts vary in perspective when describing the same event. There are no significant contradictions in the Bible that cannot be explained with that one simple truth. Jesus is worth the search. When you search for Jesus in the New Testament record, you will find a person of leadership who is hard to resist. Critical minds have examined Jesus for centuries and He is still standing while generations of skeptics have returned to dust. The manuscript, the archeological, and scientific evidence are overwhelmingly in favor of the conclusion that Jesus is not dead. Jesus did not ask death to leave Him alone; Jesus told death to leave Him alone. Jesus promises victory over death. History records that He can deliver on his promises and I am putting my total trust in His leadership. Submitting your will to His kingdom is the only way to get to know Jesus. He does not allow, "I almost submitted" or, "I was going to submit, but I just did not have time." Jesus demands your submission, warns you what will happen if you do not submit, and then lets you run your own life if you choose to.

Chapter Two

His Childhood—The Beginning of the Line

Jesus was prepared for the challenge of public ministry long before the religious leaders wanted to kill Him. His introduction as a man who would divide history goes from His birth through His childhood and on into His resurrection from the dead .

Jesus learned the harsh realities of being a dividing line early in life. He traveled with His parents to Jerusalem and found teachers who were in need of teaching. We are not sure if this is the first trip Jesus took to Jerusalem with His family. We do know He decided to stay in Jerusalem by Himself while His parents traveled a day's journey back to Nazareth. The customary route between the two cities would have taken Mary and Joseph down the Ascent of Adumin though the Wadi Kelt valley, out into Jericho and eventually to the Jordan River Valley. It is this same footpath where Jesus later taught the story of the Good Samaritan who fell among robbers. Jesus sent his parents back alone through one of the most dangerous highways of the day without the security of a caravan, just so He could stay behind in Jerusalem and visit.

No wonder Mary and Joseph were a little upset! Not only did they have the fear of not knowing about the safety of their son, they had to travel a dangerous road to find out. They had to walk uphill to get back to Jesus. The footpath from Jericho to Jerusalem is still traveled by pilgrims today. You can read the story of Jesus' visit to Jerusalem in Luke 2.

The conversation between Mary and Jesus is revealing. Luke tells us that Mary and Joseph were astonished to find Jesus in the Temple. As normal parents they may have thought Jesus might be in some kind of trouble. They were amazed to find Him in church. If either of my boys were missing I am not sure if church is the first place I would look for him. Mary seems upset when she says, "Son, why have you treated us like this?" Jesus does not apologize and plead with his mother. Jesus was a leader at the age of 12. He makes decisions that affect people. He announces that He had to be in His Father's house. In sermons I sometimes joke that this passage explains what scholars call the "years of silence" between the ages of 12 and 30. Clearly, Jesus was on restriction for his behavior toward Mom and Dad for 18 years and he was not allowed out to minister.

The point of the story is the Boy Jesus was also the King Jesus. Jesus completely understood the ramifications of his actions. He still understands the cost of following Him today. Was Jesus a nice boy? Sure, in the sense that he did not spit on children or steal sheep. Jesus was sinless because the blood that flowed through His veins was not polluted with Adam's fall. But was He nice? No. He was real; He was decisive; He was the dividing line. If the people He loved needed to be in danger in order for Him to finish, or begin,

His march to the cross, then so be it. I am convinced Jesus could have ruled the world from the time He was 12 years old. He was not the kind of kid who would ask, "Please let me lead now." He did not stand in line and wait His turn; He cut in front and asked the leaders questions they had never heard, then gave them answers beyond their understanding. Some of these same religious leaders who heard young Jesus explain Himself would later vote their approval for His death sentence.

From His Birth Jesus Has Been a Line of Division

The Christmas story we know today has major inaccuracies and omissions scattered throughout the dialogue. The actual date of Jesus' birth is unlikely to be December 25th. The Gospel of Matthew and Luke give us the historical details. Like any writer, I am inclined to fill in some of the blanks with reasonable conjecture.

All the male babies in Bethlehem were slaughtered because Jesus was born there. It is no wonder we never see Jesus in the city of his birth again according to the Biblical record. How popular would He be with the families who lost their children? If either of my sons were killed because some family from Galilee had come into town for the Census and then they never left, I might be looking for revenge.

How much hardship did these families in Bethlehem endure?

Casual readers of the New Testament think that the Wise Men came to the manger where Jesus was born. People also hold the belief that the angels were singing to the shepherds when the Bible says they spoke. As a matter of fact, there is no record of any angels singing until after the Resurrection. It is not until Revelation 5 that there is a record of angels singing, and even that passage could be translated that angels speak instead of sing. We know from the Bible that singing angels are not a part of the birth of Jesus.

The Scripture clearly teaches the Wise Men came to a house where Jesus and His parents lived. What does all this mean? It means that Joseph and Mary settled in Bethlehem for up to two years after Jesus was born. They went to the market; they met friends. Jesus played with some of the young boys who were killed. Mary knew their names. Herod had all the babies killed who were under the age of two, because Jesus could have been that old. These were cute little boys. Boys with golden skin and dark eyes. I have watched little boys play in the streets of modern Bethlehem. Like their ancestors they appeared innocent and jovial. The little boys in Jesus' neighborhood were just like the little boys in your neighborhood, that is until Herod's soldiers rode into town.

Liberal theologians try to discount much of the New Testament record. They do the same with the passages surrounding the early life of Jesus. Two thousand years of history have silenced the cries of the families in Bethlehem who lost their young sons. This massacre really happened. Herod the Great, a building tyrant who later had 10,000 people imprisoned so that upon his death in Jericho they could all be murdered, is quite capable of a *small* atrocity like this. The text also tells us not only were the male children in Bethlehem killed, but also all the children in the vicinity of Bethlehem. The little town of Bethlehem is built on a hill. From just outside the Church of the Nativity you can stand and look out over the vicinity of Bethlehem. Every home, with or without children, would have been affected by the presence of Jesus and the paranoid anger of Herod. Their screams cried out that

Jesus was the dividing line between life and death and fulfilled yet another prophecy surrounding the birth and childhood of Jesus. (Matthew 3)

Jesus has never been afraid or ashamed of being the Hard Line of Division. Jesus is not afraid of being rejected, nor is He afraid of simply stating the line upon which eternity will be measured. His life, death, burial, and resurrection is that line. If you are expecting Him to apologize for who He is and be a pleasant little leader who pleases the public, you have a little more research to do into the ramifications of His appearance in history. The manger scene is not about Christmas songs and Santa Claus. The manger announced a new Ruler. A new King. A leader to be obeyed even when questions surrounded Him. That God would bring this new royalty into a grotto with such humble beginnings only underlines how far the journey was for Jesus in the incarnation from heaven to His future coronation as King of Kings.

Even with all of this, people still think they can tell Jesus what to do. There are people in our world today who push Jesus aside and effectively tell Him to sit down and shut up. Some of these people are religious scoundrels who fleece the flock with promises of prosperity. Some of them are skeptics who paint a picture of Jesus as a pip squeak who could not skip stones across a lake, let alone walk on water. Other people universalize everything Jesus said so that He is not disagreeable to anyone. There are groups of people who follow the Gospel of Church Growth that says as long as the Church is growing, then our words and actions are unimportant. Feel-good sermons that avoid the confrontation that contemplation about Jesus produces flow from pulpits like the waterfall at my favorite golf course. Jesus did not leave Heaven to please us, He left Heaven to lead us. His birth and Childhood are a brief glimpse of the character of God and the essential importance of the doctrine of the incarnation.

Without the virgin birth and the resulting revelation of the Godhead, there is no salvation plan or Gospel story. The proclamation that God became flesh and 'pitched his tent' with us is one of the foundational doctrines defining who Jesus is. His birth and His childhood reveal a portion of His character. Without the virgin birth, Christianity would never have spread throughout the world in the first century. If Jesus is not God from before birth, then he cannot be God after death. His sacrificial death on the cross is impossible without the incarnation. If Jesus was not born of a virgin, then He is just another crucified rebel. It is ironic that the skeptics who try to discount the virgin birth would have no target without the virgin birth because Christianity would not have been possible without the sinless appearance of Jesus through the birth canal.

Having doubts about a fairy tale is different from not understanding every detail about the mystical nature of the Virgin Birth. If historical facts can be trusted concerning Alexander the Great, then those same historical facts point toward a Jesus who was not just a man.

The virgin birth is how we explain and teach about the part of Jesus that was divine.

Chapter Three

His Manhood and Ministry— The Line Underlined

One important question to ask about Jesus and His ministry is whether or not He was a nice guy. This question clarifies our image of Jesus. The answer is with out a doubt NO. Jesus was *not* a nice guy in the sense that our American culture would define the word. Jesus was then, is now, and always will be a dividing line. He is the division between what is good and what is evil. He is the division between right and wrong. Being united with Jesus puts you into a position to defend His position. If you are a nice person who thinks that Jesus was a nice person who got along with everyone at all costs, you might have a few problems with some of the positions Jesus takes in the New Testament.

For instance, Jesus teaches that He is the only way to God. That does not sound too tolerant. Jesus does not sound like a nice guy if He excludes every other religion, every other leader, every other nice guy who is just trying to give his opinion. The conclusion that Jesus is the only way to

God is actually a bedrock foundation that is taught in the New Testament doctrine of Atonement.

If you are united with Jesus because you have submitted your will to Him, then you have been imputed with His righteousness. Because He divided history on the cross you can now be called good or righteous. Your personal goodness, or badness, as the case may be, qualifies you as a loser in the righteousness game. If we were keeping score, you would always be the loser. Even if your level of goodness is way up there, I mean, even if you have never killed a flea, you are still a loser in the perfection category. The fact that you are not perfect makes you imperfect, and that imperfection makes you a loser in the game of righteousness.

The doctrine of atonement is accomplished because of the work Christ has done, not because of the work we have done. He did this work in spite of us, not with our help. The cross was not a nice place. It was a bloody, criminal, smelly, disgusting place of death and total humiliation. Nice guys do not go to a cross. Nice guys talk their way out of the cross.

The Crown or the Cross

The work of atonement was no easy task. In order to accomplish His goal, Jesus had to daily seek out a cross of humiliation and reject a crown of applause. If an earthly kingdom had been his goal, opportunities were constantly being presented to Him to accept it. But Jesus rejected the earthly crown and embraced the despised cross. A nice guy would never have made it to the cross. Nice guys do not turn over tables. Nice guys do not berate and insult political and religious leaders. Nice guys do not tell followers they must eat his flesh and drink his blood. Nice guys do not tell their best friends they will desert him and deny his work. Nice guys do not tell people that they will be judged by the standard of perfection as Jesus does in Matthew 6. The price Jesus paid for us to have a relationship with God included not being popular and nice. The price Jesus paid included speaking the truth and alienating his family and friends. The price Jesus paid included leaving Heaven and starting his air-breathing life so we could have a future after our air breathing life. If you think the work of atonement was done by a nice guy who wanted everyone to be happy and was looking for a perfect compromise then you need to read the New Testament again. The Jesus presented in the New Testament was the dividing line who was interested in the bottom line.

People died on the way to the cross, at the cross, and after the cross. Jesus is not afraid of His death or your death. Was Jesus a Nice Guy? The record seems to indicate that he was very goal-oriented and being nice does not always fit the mold of a goal-oriented person. Of course, Jesus was always righteous. He did not sin. Being Divine in nature He was able to see through pretentiousness. Jesus pushed his students to levels no other Rabbi had ever called men to before. He asked them if they thought He was Divine. If they hesitated or denied Him, then he pushed them away with words and actions. (John 6:66)

We often think because Jesus called the 12 apostles that he only had 12 disciples. He actually had many disciples. Dozens and dozens. We see this when Mathias is selected to replace Judas early in Acts. There were several candidates who had been with Jesus from the start of His public ministry until His ascension. These candidates did not include the women we are told about in Luke 8 who also faithfully followed Jesus. He chose the 12 apostles from a larger group. Nice guys do not exclude faithful followers. A nice guy would have appointed hundreds of apostles.

Several people have responded with displeasure when I have presented my view that Jesus was not a nice guy according to our American perception of niceness. There are other questions that will lead you to the same conclusion about Jesus. That is, is there anywhere in the Bible where Jesus offends people? Would it be possible to be crucified without having offended someone? Did Jesus come to fulfill our expectations or to teach us His expectations? Is it possible that a Western view of Jesus could remove his authoritative position and reduce Him to someone who does what we say? Does our idea of fairness prevent us from allowing Jesus to be the final arbitrator? Does the current culture cry of 'can't we all just get along' exclude Jesus from ruling his kingdom as he sees fit with out our input? I could go on, but I hope you get my point. The life of Jesus is not a story about how compromise and negotiation bring success. Jesus came so that we could be pleasing to God through His blood sacrifice of atonement. Jesus did not come so that he could please us or bow down to the throne of political correctness. In his day, the politically incorrect were silenced with nails. He stood up to that pressure; do you really think he will have any problem standing up to the pressure of our day?

It is impossible to be victorious with Jesus without being aligned with Jesus. And make no mistake about this fact, Jesus will be victorious with or without our submission. The preceding discourse describes the man we call Jesus presented in the historical evidence. The next step in maturity is to study what this man taught.

Chapter Four

His Teaching Ministry

The overall summary of Jesus' teaching is that if you obey the King you will be rewarded. On the other hand if you disobey the King you will be punished. Jesus is clearly the line between reward and punishment. Jesus did not comment much on the politics of His day. He restricted His presentation to the politics of His coming Kingdom. His Kingdom is ruled by a Monotheistic Dictatorship. His Kingdom has a Supreme Military Commander, not a CEO.

My wife brought a women's devotional book home one day. It had flowers on the cover. It was the kind of book you wanted to kiss before you read it. In the second chapter, the author presented her assumption that Jesus would hum songs while he traversed through the Galilee. Jesus humming through the lilies. Jesus was not a hippie humming, he was a rabbi teaching. The Bible says that they sang a hymn, not that they hummed a tune (Matt. 26, Mark 14).

People want Jesus to be like them. The reality is that Jesus is unlike anyone. He is one of a kind, never to be equaled or duplicated. Jesus is not interested in negotiating a settlement or finding the common ground so people can be comfortable. If there is one blaring truth that His message teaches us, it is to please shut up and listen. Do you think Jesus really cares about your opinion? Do you think that he cares if you *feel* like serving Him? Jesus does care and love each individual person. However, his love toward us does not excuse us to behave in immature, self-centered ways that confuse his message. The point of his teaching in the New Testament is that every individual will be held accountable for their response to the coming King. When you train your mind to welcome Jesus as a current and future ruler you will begin to treat your personal desires and needs as secondary to His. When you are presented with a problem or opportunity, you will deliberate how Jesus would want you to respond. That is called Christian maturity.

Just because Jesus spoke about love and goodness does not mean He is a wishy-washy, mamby-pamby leader who wants everyone to be happy. Jesus loves people who submit to His authority. The fact that Jesus presents his message of love to everyone and makes entrance into His kingdom available to everyone does not mean that He loves people who openly and violently reject Him in the same way He loves people who openly and honestly accept Him. Jesus loves all sinners but Jesus will also send dissenters to Judgment where they will be punished forever. Do not think for even a minute that Jesus is afraid or hesitant to send people to Judgment. He *will* repay rejection with vengeance.

His desire is that every person would repent (2 Peter 3:9). His goal is that through love people will see Him for who he is. Please, make no mistake about this, whoever rejects Jesus will be rejected by Jesus. When you accept His Divinity and His power to forgive the personal offenses that you have committed against God, then you gain entrance into life forever instead of death forever. The flip side of this coin is that Jesus is never mean. He does not threaten people with his authority and superior position. He humbly shows his power and invites all people to accept His leadership.

Saying Jesus is a nice guy is as ignorant as saying that Jesus is an American or that Jesus is a white guy. It reminds me of people who refer to God as the 'Big Guy in the Sky'. If you really want to understand Jesus, you must get away from the North American concept of leadership *and research the Middle East*. Jesus is a King, not a President. Jesus is self-appointed, not elected. Jesus does not care about the majority vote, He is the majority vote. There will be no recount with Jesus like there was in the closest election in the U.S. when George W. Bush was elected. It is not that complicated to count three votes. And the vote is unanimous. Jesus gives commands, not suggestions. We follow Jesus, He does not follow us. Jesus does not take an opinion poll, his opinion is the poll. Jesus gives orders, he does not take orders. His divine position is not open to opinion or discussion. The virgin birth, Godhead, Salvation by Grace, Resurrection of Christ and His followers, and other orthodox doctrines of the church are not open for debate. Jesus has proclaimed reality and if you disagree with Him then you will be publicly punished. (Matt. 24:50)

There is a great comfort in letting Jesus be in charge. The symptoms of our society are a result of our being in charge of ourselves. The amazing number of self-help books on the market today is a commentary on how successful we have been at being in charge of ourselves. Rich people I know are not happy because of what they own. Poor people I know are not sad because of what they do not have. It is impossible for people to successfully be in charge of their own lives. We all need divine intervention and direction.

If you honestly examine Jesus and you are open to an unbiased look at the evidence, you will find leadership that is hard to resist. The information available to anyone seeking it is overwhelming. Go to any Christian bookstore and investigate the sections that deal with apologetics. Men like Josh McDowell and Hank Hanegraaf have done primary research that can help seekers become believers. Even without the excellent work of scholars over the past 1900 years, any person is without excuse before God. The very existence of the creation will speak out against all doubters and scoffers. People who have been raped, abused, addicted, shunned, ashamed or passed over have no excuse for rejecting Jesus. People who have been endorsed, elected, embraced, enhanced or romanced have no excuse for rejecting Jesus. No excuse will stand when Jesus, 'the nice guy' is hearing your case.

I was witnessing to a man in a casino recently. We talked for about 45 minutes and the more we talked, the more angry he became. I answered each of his objections with undeniable evidence. He was playing a game called Keno which looks like Bingo. One of his arguments was that if I were not sitting there with him, then it would be impossible for him to be wrong because there would be no one to disagree with and that would make him right. He said this because Jesus had never appeared to him personally. I tried to tell him that a defense built on the premise that he was alone in the universe might not go too far with the Being who created the universe. I suggested Jesus was indeed making an appearance to him through me and that God cared about him enough to speak with him directly in a bar in a casino through one of his servants. After he finished insulting me and using various profane words to describe my family heritage, I informed him that if he continued to be abusive and reject God's plan for his life, then he would have to face the consequences of Jesus not liking him. This man rejected Jesus.

Jesus dealt with rejection, rebellion, and unbelief with the Rich Young Ruler, Nicodemus, Judas Iscariot, His brothers, His disciples, John the Baptist, Herod Antipas, Herod the Great, Pilate, His followers, and the Romans. Every other group of people he ministered to including the sick, the blind, the lame, the lepers, the rich, the poor, the political and the religious were part of the rejection he faced every day.

As I study the air-breathing life of Jesus, I am amazed at how often he did not lose his cool. Certainly there are times when Jesus seems upset, but for the most part, he handles opposition by teaching facts and sharing emotions instead of attacking His enemies peronally. This is part of what He means when He tells us to love our enemies. His students asked Him to be more forceful. His enemies challenged Him to make his case clearer. His siblings doubted Him. Yet he stays on course all the way to the cross. Do you think that His enemies were nice about their attacks on Him? Do you think they were calm and gentle when they called him a bastard and plotted to kill Him? What did they yell at Him? What new insult could they come up with in their hatred for Him? What wise cracks and teasing could they quietly have whispered to Him?

A rich Christian Businessman once shook my hand and wished me good luck in my little ministry. He was letting me know he did not really treasure my work with the homeless. How many people shook Jesus' hand and gave Him a piece of their mind? Another man once returned my business card telling me he would never need it. How many well-established, hard-working Jewish shopkeepers waved Jesus off and belittled His march to the cross? Every day Jesus faced the ridicule and the indecision of the masses.

One time I was sharing devotions with a group of Christian young men as we sat in a restaurant in Sitka, Alaska across the street from the Shee Atika Lodge. We had been there for several hours when I began witnessing to one of the drunks who was listening in on our conversation. As we talked, an older man, who had just finished dinner, rose to his feet and raising his hand, he pointed his finger at me and said, "You are an evangelistic *#?@*. Every day I come into this restaurant and I have to listen to this blankety-blank country music and I will be damned if I am going to listen to you spout off about your blanking Jesus any more." All eyes were on me as I rose and pointed my finger back at this man.

I said, "Sir, we do not mean to bother you, but since we came in here tonight you have been smoking and drinking. Now, none of us are smoking but we have had to put up with this stinking smoke for the last two hours."

The older man got a little red in the face and a little shaky on his feet when he said, "Yea, well this is a smoking Restaurant."

I thought about that for a second and then I told him, to the applause of our little group, that this was a talking restaurant too and if he did not mind, we were going to continue our discussion about the King of Kings and the Lord of Lords. If he did not like it, he could just take his smokes and hit the road. Standing up to skeptics and abusive people does not violate the teaching of Jesus because real love explains the truth.

I am not sure how Jesus felt when they held up the coin, or when he asked for someone to throw the first stone, or when Peter paid the temple tax with a coin from the mouth of a fish, but I imagine it was a little like how our group felt as we gathered around the Bible in that lonely restaurant in Sitka. Jesus was, is, and always will be the hard line between Heaven and Hell. With Him you have everything important; without Him you have nothing worthwhile.

Jesus—A Jewish Rabbi

If you want to have a deep understanding of the New Testament you need to see the written word through the eyes of a Rabbi and His students. Before they were Apostles, they were disciples. Before they were disciples, they were workers. Jesus took ordinary workers and transformed them into extraordinary world leaders. He did this with the Jewish rabbinical form of teaching. God invented the Jewish Nation. All of Jewish history culminates in Christ. Prophets, Kings, Priests, Scribes, and Teachers are all God's idea. God's overall plan of redemption includes them in a painted picture that gives an example of who the Messiah would be.

Jesus fulfilled all of the Messianic prophecies. He proved that He was the Son of God (Divine) and the Son of Man (Human). As a rabbi, Jesus used parables and object lessons to bring his students to the point where they could recognize Him as the Saving Messiah. One of His big problems was trying to convince them that His Kingdom was not of this world but of the world to come. The students finally got the truth of this lesson somewhere between the

Resurrection and Pentecost. The Biblical record teaches that they expected Jesus to return during their lifetime.

There are overwhelming examples in the New Testament that show Jesus teaching as a Rabbi. When He teaches about sheep, wine, figs, wheat, rulers, widows, seeds, or giving, praying, fasting, loving, serving, healing, building, asking, following, and faith, the objects of His lesson were always close by.

We have an incredible example of this in John 4. Jesus has his group of uneducated students in the very unrabbinical location of Samaria. They come upon Jacob's well in the Old Testament city of Sychar. This is the only location in the book of John that I have not been able to visit because of the current political unrest surrounding this site. The political unrest preventing some tourist groups from seeing Jacob's well was alive and active in Jesus' day as well. Upon coming to the well, his students went into town to get provisions while Jesus conversed with a Samaritan woman. Although it is interesting, if you only concentrate on the discourse between Jesus and the woman, you will miss the main point that the Apostle John is trying to make.

The disciples leave the city with food but no followers. Meanwhile the woman leaves Jesus in a hurry, possibly because of the approaching men, and runs to the same city the disciples just left in order to tell the people in town she thinks she has found the Messiah. The anticipation of the Messiah was very high in the holy land in 30 AD. Many people from that town believed in Christ (John 30:39) They came out to Him from the same town the disciples had just left. While they were coming, Jesus told His students to, "Open your eyes and look at the fields! The fields are ripe for harvest." What do you think they were looking at? Jesus the Rabbi was teaching another object lesson. Here comes the field! The field is a bunch of half-breed Samaritan rejects who the disciples just saw in town and now they are storming out of town toward Jesus. Jesus is teaching the future world leaders that racial status has no bearing in His Kingdom.

If they want to follow Him, they need to be ready to share the message with anyone who will listen and with many who will not. Over the past twenty years in my work with the poor, I have been shot at, kicked at, swung at, and cussed at by every racial group on the streets. I have also been prayed for, paid by, and sent out by every racial group. The heart has no color. Jesus is interested in your attitude. Jesus wants to teach you. Can you see the fields? Samaria made it into the Great Commission in Acts 1. Peter was given a refresher course about this same issue in Acts 10. The book of Jonah underlines this same message, and the apostle Paul later clarifies this issue with Peter. The Acts 15 Council is directly related to race and ethnic background. Jesus made no distinction with regard to race, color, sex or background.

Jesus does not care about anyone's ethnic origin. He does not care about anyone's religious background or moral history. He simply asks for unconditional surrender to Him. When someone is united with Christ by turning his or her life over to Him with total abandon, then Jesus becomes a nice guy to them. When racist and small-minded red necks in white robes ignore Jesus and arrogantly claim that He endorses their insanity, then Jesus becomes a guy who will be anything but nice to them.

Martin Luther King is one of the greatest men who has ever lived. He may have had moral problems just like the rest of us, but he understood that Jesus does not look at the color of someone's skin to judge them. MLK went to be with Jesus when he was assassinated. Heaven will be filled with every race from every nation. If you have any problems with this discussion, you should read John 4 more carefully.

Chapter Five

The Rabbi Teaches

The Gospels are filled with examples of Jesus teaching as a Rabbi. Seeing Jesus as a Rabbi may shed some light on the passage where Jesus teaches that God can move mountains. If the disciples were on the Mount of Olives when Jesus was teaching this, they would have been able to see the Herodian in the distance. The Herodian was an escape fortress built by Herod the Great and while it looks much like Massada, it is closer to Jerusalem. To build this fortress, Herod had his slave labor actually move a mountain to the top of a nearby hill. The result is a rather strange tower with a mountain that is shaved in half right by its side. Jesus the Rabbi may have been teaching that if you need a mountain moved in your life, God may just hand you a shovel. Understanding that Jesus spoke using idioms of the Aramaic language is essential to understanding some of what he said. In English if we say someone is in 'hot water' we know not to take it literally. Jesus used idioms and object lessons His followers would easily understand. This may have been one of them.

Here are two other quick examples of how Jesus taught using object lessons while living eyeball to eyeball with his students. In John 5 and 9 there are two occasions where Jesus heals a social outcast. In the John 5 passage, we see that Jesus healed an undeserving, back-stabbing snitch who not only makes excuses for his condition, but seems to want to stay crippled so that he can continue to make a living as a beggar by the pool. If there was ever a search to find the man with the worst character in the New Testament, this man would be a leading candidate. If you carefully read this passage, you will find that he eventually turns Christ over to the authorities who are trying to develop a case to accuse Christ of treason and blasphemy. I believe that this man turned on Christ in a worse way than Judas. Certainly, situations like this prepared Christ for the future betrayal of Judas. John 5 is a mini-cross type experience for Jesus and an incredible object lesson for His disciples. In John 5, the Pharisees and enemies of Christ get their first look at what they hope will be a future trial. Jesus then spends the rest of the chapter telling them who He will call for His witnesses. This lesson would come down hard on the disciples. Jesus would stand up to Religion. Jesus has witnesses who will testify for Him. Will you betray him or stand with Him? A more complete exegesis of John 5:5 reveals that this crippled man had been by the pool for 38 years. That is a long time to sit by a pool being turned away.

Most of the street people I know would have no problem negotiating some type of settlement in far fewer than 38 years. I once knew a street man named Gene who had no legs. He spent his days foraging through back alleys at the Pike Place Market in Seattle gathering discarded produce and food. He would then wheel them around in his chair selling them to tourists and would often bring our mission goodies for our staff to enjoy. (The pastries were our favorite!) Gene would not have been lying at the pool for 38 years.

In John 5:7, the same lame man is making excuses for his long stay instead of accepting responsibility for himself, then in verse 11 we have him blaming others instead of admitting to his part in Jesus' alleged crime of healing on the Sabbath. Finally in verse 15 we see him rolling over on Jesus which increased the already present desire of the leaders to kill Jesus in verse 18. This is not a pretty picture to paint of this new friend of Jesus. Our Western world trains us to believe that anyone with a disability is ingrained with instant superior moral fiber. Moral content has deeper roots than physical liabilities. Just because the man in John 5 was lame, does not mean that he was on the moral up and up. His actions reveal his character and the outcome of the story, namely the persecution of Jesus, expose his true intentions.

In John 9, we see almost the complete opposite. Jesus heals a man who was born blind. This man loves Jesus. He defends Jesus in not just one trial, but two. Against the strength and power of the culture and religion of his day, he holds his ground for his healer. The beggar in John 5 does not even know who healed him. The blind man in John 9 not only knows it was Jesus who healed him, but he gives up any future privilege of worship in the Temple because he believes Jesus is a Prophet.

As a blind beggar, he could not go to the Temple. He had been looked down on his whole life. He was a sinner from birth in the eyes of organized religion. Jesus cleansed him and made him a candidate for Temple Worship. This blind man got a better deal. In one of the most emotional passages in the Gospels he worships Jesus because he sees Jesus as not just as a Rabbi, not just as a healer, not just as a friend. He worships Jesus as the Divine Son of God.

Jesus used this incredible occurrence to show his disciples and his enemies how blind they were. This is irony at its best; healing a blind man to show others how their actions are blind moralism. That is the heart of rabbinical teaching. Jesus was not only a Jewish rabbi, He was an extremely good Jewish rabbi. Both of these healings were intentionally performed on the Sabbath as if to underline the lesson that Jesus was the author of the law as well as the keeper of the law.

In his great book, *The Jesus I Never Knew*, Phillip Yancey spends an entire chapter on the Jewishness of Jesus.[1] He would tell you in a nice way what I would tell you bluntly. Jesus was Jewish for a reason. If you don't like it, lump it. God did not ask your opinion regarding when, where, or how He sent His son. Furthermore, Jesus was a Rabbi for a reason. If you do not study Him for who He is, you will miss major portions of what He teaches.

Jesus is the hard line between teaching and learning. If you refuse to be taught you will never learn. We are living in a know it all culture. Information speeds around the globe, but is anyone really learning anything? Just because you can repeat facts does not mean you have learned anything. Jesus never gave a test in the classroom sense of the word. He never wrote anything down as far as we know. He asked his followers to come to a conclusion based on the evidence of what they saw and heard. Jesus taught a small group to teach a small group to then again teach another small group. Then, after His final object lesson of the Resurrection, He got all these small groups together to form the early Church. They then modeled His teaching method and the Church exploded throughout the world in the First Century.

The One-on-One-No-Building-Required Church Model

Why have we abandoned the model of teaching that Jesus used? When Paul, a first century Apostle of Jesus, tells the church in Ephesians 4:11 that some are Apostles, some Prophets, some Evangelists, some Pastors and some Teachers, he is letting us know that it is Jesus who sets this up to prepare God's people for works of Service. Paul understood that Jesus was a Rabbi. Paul had been trained by a Rabbi. Do you think Paul was suggesting some new radical model that did not include one-on-one rabbinical teaching? I doubt it.

Several years ago I did a study using a Harmony of the Gospels. A Harmony is simply the events of Jesus' life laid out in chronological order side by side in each gospel account. Of the 108 events occurring in the early ministry, the Galilean ministry, and the Judean and Perean ministry of Jesus, circa AD 27–30, only ten events took place with Jesus inside conventional religious buildings. Jesus was not inside a religious building all the time. He was in the synagogue less than ten percent of the time. The Apostles did not stay in the church building 90 percent of the time and go on mission trips ten percent of the time. Just the opposite. They learned from their Rabbi to go out and challenge people with the gospel. If Paul had stayed in the church building he never would have left on a missionary journey. If Jesus was only in an organized place of religion ten percent of the time, if the Apostles were not sitting around in church most of the time, then why are we? We have somehow lost the Rabbinical model that Jesus taught. He sent them OUT.

Before He sent them out, He went out with them. That is the core of discipleship. Are you willing to follow the Rabbi out into a world full of competition, questions, and doubt? Are you willing to lead others by your flawed transparent example?

The Church is where we go to get the game plan, not to play the game. The world is not watching us inside the church building. We have mistakenly come to the conclusion that a good worship time is the extent of our Christian Service. There is even a new buzz word called Worship Evangelism. I am convinced Jesus would not stay to long in our churches any more than he stayed very long in their churches. I see Him coming in the front door and asking anyone who is serious about their faith to leave with Him out the back door. Jesus might even leave in the middle of a good worship song and God forbid He interrupt our worship! This is an important question, do we really need all our church buildings?

Let's leave it here. Jesus was a Jewish rabbi who claimed to be God's Divine Son and proved it with wonderful works and words. Your involvement with Him now is not independent of who He was then or who He is now. Discipleship is going out into a world opposed to Christ with the message of Christ. Sitting in church and listening to sermons is not discipleship. Hearing God's word preached by a called pastor is a wonderful experience, but if that is the extent of your Christian experience, then you are missing some of the most important messages in the Bible.

In closing Part One of this book, let me tell you about the story of Jenny. She was raised in a middle class home in the suburbs of Seattle. She was born in 1960 and her early years were a commentary on the sweeping cultural changes of Sex, Drugs, and Rock & Roll. There were little boys in the neighborhood where she grew up who made fun of Jenny. This no doubt left scars on Jenny. She battled with her weight and with depression. In 1988, she was raped by two men in South Seattle. Two years later, Jenny tested positive for the AIDS virus. Eighteen months later she was confined to her bed at the Bailey-Bushe AIDS Hospice. I visited with Jenny there at the aids hospice for three days and during that time, I did very little but pray for her. I shared a booklet with her written by Jay Carty called *Only Tens Go to Heaven*. I talked with Jenny about how Jesus could make her a perfect TEN with God and I clearly remember she told me she had never been a 'ten' before. When she confessed Christ and accepted Him as her Redeemer, I did not know how close to death she was. On the fourth day when I came to meet with Jenny, I had a lot I wanted to share with her because, you see, I was one of those little boys in her neighborhood.

Jenny died that morning. I cried for the pain, but I was glad that the Rabbi Jesus had forgiven her just like He had forgiven me. People do not physically die in church. That is why Jesus spent 90% of His time in the hospitals.

Part Two

Jesus: The Line Between The Church and The Kingdom

The Leader of the Next 1000 Years

The major battle between Christianity and the spiritual world is the difference between a religion that ruins mankind and a relationship that restores mankind. The religion that ruins us is a vast variety of systems that teach us how we can work our way into favor with God. From fundamental Roman Catholic heresies to Fundamental Islamic atrocities and back through Mormonism or Hinduism, these religions spell death for mankind. Religions hurt people. Religion is wrong. Religion does not please God. There is nothing that you can do with or without religion to bring yourself into a right relationship with God. He is not impressed with you. You will always get a failing grade in the test of character if you stand before God without a relationship with Jesus. It does not matter how much you strive, connive, bargain, or convince, work, give, sacrifice, or barter, God is not impressed with your accomplishments outside the finished work of Christ.

Mormonism would love to be recognized as Christian. Their doctrine of works for salvation, among the other heresies they endorse, disqualifies them from following Christ on His terms. Following Christ on your own terms is one aspect of being a religious idiot and is duplicated throughout history in many different cults and religions.

The finished work of Christ provides a place where followers or disciples of Jesus can meet to share the burdens of the ongoing fight against a religious world that will never accept salvation as a gift. This is called the church. The actual meaning of the word is simply *the called out ones*. My attitude toward this organization called the church has changed through the years. In my early Christian years, I clung to the church like a baby kangaroo in its mother's pouch. After Bible college and ordination, there was a slow hesitation and eventually a submerged anger with the church. It was during this time I embarked on a study that drastically changed my outlook on the only organization Jesus left behind. This study produced eleven distinctions between the Church of Christ and the Kingdom of Christ. Both the Kingdom and the Church belong to Christ. They are His. Jesus is the line of distinction between these two possessions of His. Anger toward the Church is not uncommon. People have been burned by religion and they blame the Church. God helped me in a great way to appreciate and protect the Church by looking at how the Bible presents The Church and The Kingdom as separate, but related organizations.

In an effort to help the church be the church Christ wants it to be, let me give you the four main distinctions.

Chapter Six

The Church is Temporary . . . The Kingdom is Eternal

The Church is the Bride of Christ. Being a bride is a temporary condition, because the bride is in the process of becoming the wife. Ask any newly married man if his bride is different from his wife and you will begin to understand the distinction between the temporary condition that the Church has been in since the arrival and departure of Christ and the permanent or eternal nature of His Kingdom. The engaged bride will go through the ceremony and enter into the Kingdom.

The Kingdom of God existed before the church. When the church structure ends, the Kingdom will still be in existence. The Kingdom of God will never end and Jesus the King will rule forever.

There has been a great debate going on for over 1500 years about what Augustine called the visible and the invisible church. Through the centuries, different theologians have modified Augustine's original thought that there was a church you could see that contained both saved and unsaved people, or wheat and chaff, and a church you could not see, which was made up of only truly saved people. Modern scholars (Schleiermacher, Ritschl, Barth,) try to define the church with different connections to Christ using great big fancy words. How about this instead? The Church is made up of air-breathing followers of Christ; if you are not breathing air anymore, but you accepted Christ then that means you are a dead Christian. That would make you a part of the eternal Kingdom, yet still a member of the Church. This produces the visible members who are still breathing air and the invisible members who are physically dead, but spiritually still members.

Another way to say it might be that the called-out ones will one day be the called-up ones. Until the day when the church is called to the marriage ceremony, we are taught in Scripture to remain in the world and continue to be a representation of who Christ is within the Church. We are to not become weary in well-doing and while letting our light shine before men we are salt and light to the World. When we are angry with the Church because that organization does not meet our expectations, maybe we should realize the limitations of the temporary organization called the church and place those expectations of perfection onto an organization that actually is eternal—His Kingdom.

If you go to any ice cream store you will find more than one flavor. The store offers more than one flavor because people buy more than one flavor. People enjoy more than one flavor. Inside the parameter of organized, orthodox, doctrinally-solid, Biblically-correct expressions of the Church there is room for more than one flavor. God likes variety. Look at creation; it is full of variety. There are forty thousand different varieties of beetles. Why would we think that God would want only one flavor of Church? Why would we think people would want only one flavor of Church? Organizations that are not doctrinally-solid or Biblically-correct do not qualify to be called The Church. Ultimately Jesus is the line dividing the imposter religions of the world and the authentic orthodox expressions of Christianity. While He will decide who leaves the temporary Church and enters the eternal Kingdom, that departure can originate from different destinations.

Max Lucado shared a brilliant analogy of this at the Promise Keepers Clergy Conference in Atlanta, Georgia in 1996. My recollection of the story is this. Max said that all Christians are on the same boat. This vessel leaves the harbor every day searching for people who are lost at sea and in danger of drowning and losing their lives. This Christian vessel is supposed to be about the business of saving lives, but it is soon apparent that the shipmates are much too busy fighting and quarreling among themselves to bother with anyone who is not already on board.[2]

As I see this played out in the church of our day, it is not long before some people on board become sick or wounded and leadership decides to throw them overboard. Is it any wonder why some people feel burned by the church? It will be a great day when the Christian vessel pulls into its eternal harbor in God's Kingdom. Hang on my Christian friend, someday we will arrive.

The temporary nature of the Church produces a building construction and maintenance problem for students of Jesus. All of the buildings we are pouring our resources into are temporary structures that will never enter the Kingdom of God. There are many Christians who suffer from facility sickness. The building construction and maintenance becomes more important than the original reason the building was built. It is easier to be committed to a building you can see, than it is to a Savior you cannot see. There is no building budget in Heaven. There are no donor campaigns requiring a pledge of commitment. If you find yourself too busy with the facility of the church you may be losing interest in the Founder of the Church. That is not going to go over well when you get to the eternal Kingdom. We should spend our time working on things that last into eternity rather than things that are temporal (2 Corinthians 4:18).

Jesus was not kidding when He said you could store up treasures in Heaven.

Chapter Seven

The Church is Sinful . . . The Kingdom is Sinless

The Church is sinful; the Kingdom is sinless. There is incredible freedom in this thought. The church is a place where people who make mistakes meet together. The church is a place where people who get angry meet together. The church is a place where people who sin, lie, cheat, lust, steal, belittle, bemoan, whine, bitch, fight, bite, and scream meet together. The church is a place where sin still exists.

You do not lose your depravity when you confess Christ. You do not lose your ability or propensity to sin when you confess Christ. When you confess Christ you enter into his eternal Kingdom and become a member of his imperfect, temporary church. Whether or not you admit it, you are a sinful, disobedient, self-centered, rebel before God. Everyone is. I can think of dozens of blatant sins that I have committed since confessing Christ. I have totally rebelled against what is good and right and sought my own prideful, lustful ways. God does not have to waste a lot of ink in the Bible to convince me that I need a Savior. Many people are not like me. They feel good about themselves because of their position, or their family heritage, or the fact that they have never killed anyone else. Have they ever lied? Have they cheated? Have they spoken unkind words or had lustful thoughts? Have they ever been jealous or envied what someone else has accomplished? Are they proud about their own accomplishments? Have they ever taken God's name in vain or broken even one of the ten commandments? Have they ever screamed obscenities or hated another person? Have they ever been drunk or high and done something to hurt someone's feelings? For that matter, have they ever hurt someone's feelings when they were sober?

It is not just the convicted killer or child molester who is a sinner. We are all sinners. Committing sin is like chipping a wind shield in your car. One chip and the windshield is completely ruined. Some people think that they are not sinners because they come from a Christian family. That makes as much sense as saying being born in a garage makes you a car or walking into a donut shop makes you a police officer. You can not become free from your sins through osmosis.

There is no perfect church because their are no perfect people. The Kingdom is where you will find perfection and relief from the sin nature. If you try to force the Church to be the Kingdom, you will increase your frustrations with an already imperfect situation.

The doctrine of sanctification has two aspects. One is called *positional* sanctification. This is the Biblical teaching that the believer is perfected in Christ. Because of the finished work of Christ on the cross, we are looked upon by God as forgiven and blameless. The second aspect of sanctification is the *process* of actually becoming holy. In the

Church we are in the process of sanctification, while in the Kingdom we have a position of sanctification. Both are true at the same time. Godly men take the time and effort to purify themselves here on earth in the temporary, sinful church.

Know-it-alls like to talk about sanctification without applying it. Lazy people love to think about sanctification, but never do anything to move toward it. Our sinful condition should not hinder us from trying to live holy lives and to separate ourselves from impurity. Ultimately holiness will have victory in the Eternal Kingdom. Until then, we are commanded to keep fighting evil and impurity in ourselves and others. We do this in the Church, through the Church, and because of the Church. Hopefully your appreciation of the church will increase as you consider these truths.

People often complain that God should lower His standards. Good people should be allowed to be with God. Why is God so picky with the entrance requirements into Heaven? Well, let's imagine that God does lower his standards. How fair would that be? Wouldn't the pedophile who only had one victim look better than the mass murderer or a rapist with 124 victims? Should the thief who just stole money be compared to a terrorist who bombs a building and kills innocent children? Maybe the standard should be lowered to let one thief into Heaven. Maybe the child rapist with just one victim can come in, but if he has two or three victims, then that is too many.

Where would you draw the line? What possible line is there besides perfection if we are still going to call heaven a better place than earth? As far as I am concerned, if you let one thief into heaven, or one rapist, that would ruin heaven for me. Imagine how God, who is holy and just, would feel about letting imperfection into his perfect empire?

Perfection is the Biblical standard and the only way to obtain perfection is to hide in the finished work of Christ. If you want to stand in front of judgment with your own flawed goodness on display, then you can. But there is another way and that is the way of the cross.

Jesus taught about wheat and tares in Matthew 13:24–30, 36–43. He teaches that the world is made up of Kingdom wheat or fruit and evil tares or empty heads. He is not teaching about dandelions in the wheat field. It would be easy to spot a dandelion in the middle of wheat. You will have a much harder challenge identifying tares among the wheat because a tare looks like wheat. The disciples were all familiar with the similarities. It is possible the Rabbi even had an example of both wheat and tares with Him while He spoke. The only difference between wheat and tares is one has the kernels of a harvest and the other has only chaff. The tare and resulting chaff has no market value while the wheat with its fruit is a cash crop.

The imperfect church may also have unsaved tares within the fold. Not only is the church filled with imperfect sinners but there may also be a percentage of unregenerate hypocrites who call the church home. The accusations of non-believers that people who go to church are no better than they are is absolutely true.

Since Jesus did not specifically apply the tares to the church in this passage, we must be careful in how we interpret this particular parable. However, there is a more applicable parable in Matthew 25. In this parable, Jesus teaches that there are ten virgins all waiting for the bridegroom to arrive, but not all of the ten virgins are prepared for his arrival. 50% or five out of ten of these future wives are late for the wedding and are eventually rejected by the groom because of their lack of preparation.

The rejection referred to in both these parables is the same. Jesus is talking about eternal punishment for those who try to fake their way into the Kingdom. In the Kingdom of Christ, there are no tares, no fakes, no hypocrites, and no sinners, only people who used to be tares, fakes, hypocrites, and sinners, but who are now washed clean by the sacrifice of Christ.

Chapter Eight

The Church Needs Money . . . The Kingdom is Paid in Full

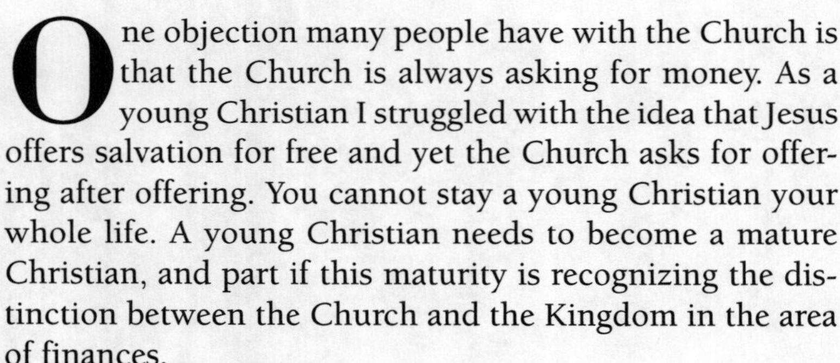

One objection many people have with the Church is that the Church is always asking for money. As a young Christian I struggled with the idea that Jesus offers salvation for free and yet the Church asks for offering after offering. You cannot stay a young Christian your whole life. A young Christian needs to become a mature Christian, and part if this maturity is recognizing the distinction between the Church and the Kingdom in the area of finances.

The subject of Jesus and money is complicated. The fact that Jesus did not place a high priority on money is underlined in the description the Apostle John gives about the financial accountability system Jesus used. This description is in the Gospel of John chapter 12. Before we summarize this passage, let's first look at where Jesus got the money He needed to travel as a Rabbi. Luke 8:3 tells us that the women who traveled with Him gave Him money from their private finances so the travelling expenses of the Rabbi and his followers could be met.

This passage in Luke is interesting because it tells us that Joanna, the wife of Herod's steward was giving money to Jesus so He could continue His ministry (Luke 8:3). Chuza, Joanna's husband, would have been in charge of the entire estate of Herod Antipas. This was a vast estate that he inherited from his father Herod the Great. It was Herod the Great who murdered the infants in Bethlehem in an attempt to stop the future ministry of King Jesus and now his estate was paying for part of the very ministry he tried to prevent. His estate paid to pave the way for King Jesus to get to the cross. Herod Antipas, one of the sons of Herold the Great, was the Herod who was involved in the crucifixion of Jesus. It is ironic and comical that both of these powerful political leaders fought against Christ when in fact they unknowingly helped to fund His ministry. It is also interesting that we do not have a list of those men who were contributing to the physical needs of The Lord. We are indebted to these women listed in Luke 8. Their reward will be great. Interestingly, Herod the Great was a contemporary of Mark Antony and Cleopatra and is mentioned in numerous writings of Josephus, a first century historian.

In John 12 we find that the funds for Jesus' ministry were kept in a money bag (John 12:6). John tells us that Judas, who managed the money used to pilfer funds from the bag. Judas did not steal everything in the bag. He just skimmed off the top. Perhaps if someone gave 10 denarii, Judas would report that someone had just made a sacrificial gift of 8 denarii. Jesus was not stupid; He knew what Judas was up to. Yet, King Jesus did not replace him or rebuke him. Jesus left a thief in charge of His financial ministry. This should teach us something about how Jesus views money. As the president of a non-profit ministry, I am trained to scrutinize every dollar. There is no way we would leave a thief in charge of our finances. Yet King Jesus did!

A debate has long raged among scholars about what Judas could have been doing with the funds he pilfered. Perhaps he was trying to buy weapons so that the coming insurrection he anticipated Jesus would lead would have the necessary equipment to overthrow the Roman government and the Jewish hierarchy. Whatever the case, Jesus was not hesitant to collect money, spend money, and in the case of Judas, even abuse money.

There are several lessons to learn from these simple passages. The first is that the Church does not need to apologize for asking committed Christians to give. The world will always find a reason to be disgruntled with the Church. Money is not the issue; stewardship is.

The second lesson is that we are often too concerned with financial goals and giving campaigns. We monitor our spiritual depth by the thickness of our bank accounts. We fall into the same trap that enslaved the Pharisees of the first century. We somehow think that our financial situation is related to God's blessing. From the sickening message of the current prosperity gospel to the idea that God looks down on poor people, we 21st century Christians have a twisted view of money. I wonder if Jesus ever really knew, or even cared how much money was in the money bag? I seriously cannot imagine Jesus being concerned with the account total or even who gave how much. He had much more important things on His mind. Jesus is the hard line between money on earth and riches in Heaven.

This brings us to another lesson about financial matters and that is the importance we place on money. Money does indeed make the world go 'round, but it is God who rotates the Earth. We are a part of a world system that is fueled by money, yet Jesus explicitly teaches us that His Kingdom is not of this world, so money is not important in His Kingdom. The streets in the new Jerusalem are made of gold. The dust on your feet in Heaven will be gold dust. Money is meaningless in God's economy and the Church is a part of that economy.

Jesus taught that the economy in His Kingdom was based on storage of true riches in Heaven. It is possible to have an eternal retirement account. Jesus taught that His economy was based on future rewards not immediate financial gains. There is a supernatural currency.

Jesus taught in Mark 12:41–44 that the sacrificial giving of money is based on percentages. The poor widow gave all she had to live on or 100% of her finances. Others gave large sums of money, but Jesus said this poor widow gave more than any of them. The widow's mite is a small copper coin approximately the size of a penny, which was issued by the Roman government and worth a fraction of a cent in Jesus' day. Today, tourists can buy a widow's mite in the Holy Land for between four and twenty dollars. The widow in Mark 12 put two such coins into the offering, and they were the only two coins she had. I would not suggest you become proud and boastful of all the giving you have done until you have met the standard set by this poor widow. Have any of us put all we have into the offering?

The Lessons From Widows

I have known several incredible widows throughout my ministry. When I became a Christian in 1977, I was living in the basement apartment of a widow's home. She was a wonderful women who drove herself to church until she was over 90 years old. I knew a widow by the name of Georgia Lamb and even presided over her memorial service after she passed away. Georgia was a model for the Pantagious Theater in the early 1920's when she made $15 an hour. She saved her money and eventually purchased a farm with her husband on Beacon Hill in Seattle. Throughout the depression years she fed needy, hungry men from outside her back door. She and her husband raised six sons of their own and 52 foster boys on their farm.

Several hundred people attended Georgia's funeral service. People from her past stood up and recounted dozens of stories about her sacrificial life. She gave away more than money. She gave her time and her love and truly gave of herself. The last time I spoke to Georgia I asked her how she would like to be remembered by her family. She told me she could put it into three words: Trust In God!

When my wife and I were first married, we lived next door to a lonely widow named Susan. Susan lived in the same house for 47 years, most of those years alone. Her husband died at a young age and she had only one living relative. My wife and I were among her only friends. Just after Susan's 92nd birthday, she became ill and died shortly thereafter. I was asked by her sister-in-law to perform the funeral. Only her sister-in-law and I stood at her graveside. I prayed and she cried, then as we walked back up the hill to leave, a car came flying into the parking lot and a harried middle-aged man ran into the funeral home. Moments later, he sprinted out to us and asked if he was too late for Susan's service. I looked at Susan's only other friend and told him we were just then on our way down to the service. The three of us walked to the graveside and I asked the workers to step aside. I prayed and the sister-in-law cried some more, then we went back up the hill to our cars.

Susan was a good person. She had given to the church and had blessed my family more than I can say, but who do you think gave more, Susan, Georgia, or the poor widow in Mark 12? More importantly, which widow are you like? How many people will remember you when you die? What have you sacrificed?

My wife and I had just brought our firstborn home from the University of Washington Hospital Neo-Natal Intensive Care Unit. He was born at 28 weeks and weighed 2 pounds, 4 ounces. At one end of the hospital it was legal to abort a child at this stage and at the other end of the hospital doctors were doing all they could to save our son's life.

We were young missionaries in those days, often with meager finances. My wife told me several weeks after our son came home from his six-week stay in the hospital that we needed diapers and food, but that our checking account was already overdrawn. As a concerned father I told her not to worry about it and I instructed her to go to the store and write a check. I told her I was not sure how, but I would come home with enough money to take care of what we needed. My wife had known me before I was a Christian. I had been arrested in three states before I was nineteen. When I told her that I would come home with money, she began to pray that I would not do something foolish that would get me arrested again. I had God on my mind that morning as I went to the Skid Road mission where I ministered for eleven years. I asked our secretary if she could double check our books to see if any support funds had come in for us that had not yet been distributed. Within an hour, she discovered $60 that a donor had sent in that I had not received. With this check in my hand, I was eager to get to the bank so I would not have to pay any of those nasty NSF fees.

On my way out the door, a homeless guy stopped me and gave me a twenty dollar bill. He told me I had let him borrow money a year earlier and he wanted to repay me. While I was standing at the chapel door, the phone rang and our secretary told me an older woman had called and wanted to donate some clothes to the mission. Her husband died a year earlier and she hoped someone could use his clothes. I quickly got her address before I headed for the bank.

Outside, my friend, Don nearly hit me with his car as he pulled over to get my attention. Don climbed out of his car and came to shake my hand. He said that the Lord had been impressing upon him to take out a ten dollar share each month in our ministry. He asked if it would be ok if he wrote a check for a his support for one year and since he was not that good about sending money he also wanted to pay for a year in advance. He wrote me a support check for $240. I was really ready to get to the bank now. To be honest with you, I was even thinking about taking my wife out for dinner.

On the way to the bank, I stopped by the widow's house to pick up the clothes she wanted to donate. She invited me in for a cup of coffee and even though I was in a hurry to cover any checks my wife had written, I settled into one of her chairs and listened to the story of her life. An hour or so later when I was picking up the small bag of clothes she had ready for me to take back to the mission, she asked if I would wait for just a moment longer. Waiting at her front door, I could see her through a crack in her bedroom door. She was on her knees in prayer. In a few moments, she returned and told me that the Lord had instructed her to give me some money. As she pushed bills into my hand, she said it was not much, but it was all she had and God had told her to give it to me. I still cry when I tell this story. I have actually had the widow's mite in my hand.

When you look back on your life, which widow do you want to be compared to? The only time we have to sacrifice is now. You will not be issued another life so you can begin to give then. In the church we have the incredible opportunity to sacrifice our lives for HIM. In the Kingdom, we will only be able to recount our sacrifices.

Money is an amazing gift to give away. The church and many para church organizations need money to continue their ministries. We should never apologize when we request finances and we must treat every gift as though it was the widow's mite.

Imagine you are standing in a line. Like most lines, it is moving. You realize where the front of this line is by what direction everyone is headed. The line is so wide you cannot see the sides. Soon the line behind you is so long you cannot see the end. All around you are thousands of people from every where in the world. You hear every language and see every race. Word comes back from the front of the line that this is the line of accounting. This news creates quite a stir around you and you ask someone close by what the line of accounting is? An old widow finally helps you by telling you that this is the line where Jesus asks you to account for your life. She walks with you in the crowd for awhile and you ask her all about her life. She tells you that she was a widow in Jerusalem for many years during the time that the Messiah walked on earth and that she became a Christian after the resurrection. She tells you that she has never seen the Messiah up close and cannot wait to meet Him. You realize this is the widow from Mark 12.

You have two thoughts. One is that Jesus might remember this widow and that her reward in Heaven will be really big. The other is that you will be giving an account of your life right after she does. Would that be good news for you?

Heaven's Refund

Do you think the widow will arrive at judgment and be given a refund? Do you think Jesus will say to Billy Graham or John Wesley or Blaise Pascal that they actually gave too much of their lives away and their storage account in Heaven is to full? Maybe it is possible to give too much, but I doubt it.

Any act of kindness, any unselfish gesture, any financial gift, any prayer offered, any shelter or food, any visit or kind word, any sacrifice large or small, all will be rewarded. An old hymn puts it like this: "your only life will soon be past, only what is done for Christ will last."[3]

Your Money . . . His Kingdom

God's Kingdom is not dependent upon your financial gifts to continue to exist. God clearly does not need your money and His Kingdom will go on forever with or without your participation. You can not pay for Grace because there is no way you could ever afford Grace. Entrance into the Kingdom is completely paid for by King Jesus. One distinction between the Kingdom and the Church is defined by how Christ used money. He is the dividing line between poverty and prosperity. He is the giver of all that is good. He will be the final accountant over our finances. Our entrance into His Kingdom is paid by Him but then he asks us to surrender ownership of everything we have to His Lordship so that His Kingdom will expand to reach more souls. These new souls need a 'called out place' to come and that place is the

Church. This Church needs to be financed by our sacrificial gifts. There is a mystical connection between the Church and the Kingdom. At the same time, there are complicated distinctions between the two. An understanding of both the similarities and distinctions can remedy many of the frustrations and complaints against the Church. Forcing the Church to behave like the Kingdom is like asking a two-year old to rip a phone book in half.

Another sidebar to the money dilemma in the church is the "holier-than-thou" attitude financial success can sometimes bring. This "holier-than-thou" attitude is produced by fostering competition in worship, preaching, giving, singing, or serving.

In Christ we have a position of holiness, but in life we work through the process of being holy. If our position in Christ produces spiritual arrogance, then the process of becoming holy is brought to a grinding halt. James, the earthly brother of Jesus, tells the early Church that God opposes the proud but gives grace to the humble (James 4:6). James was very familiar with the "holier-than-thou" attitudes of his day. Looking on the outward appearance of others and putting on an air of spiritual superiority is a disgusting practice. Jesus had an ongoing battle with the religious leaders of His day. These leaders looked down on most of the population seeing them as dirty and spiritually illiterate. The Pharisees, Sadducees, Lawyers, and Scribes had quite a surprise when Jesus ate and drank with tax gatherers and sinners (Luke 5, 6, 7,15). Jesus kept stirring up controversy with the high minded religious leaders when he healed the "sinful" beggars, crippled, blind, adulterous and deceased (John 5, 8, 9, 11).

When Jesus was confronted with the practice of defiling the table by not teaching his disciples to wash their hands properly, He taught that the real issue of cleanliness is an issue of the heart (Matthew 15). God has cleansed our hearts in Christ. We should not pollute this cleansing by giving the impression of exclusivity. "Holier than-thou" attitudes tend to elevate one group of followers above another by allowing spiritual competition in worship or gifts to become the goal rather than living a holy life. Certainly the process of holiness includes separating ourselves from sinful behavior and thoughts; it does not include elevating yourself above other Christians or being shocked by the presence of sin in the unbelieving world. We should expect the unbelieving world to be filled with sin; that is why we call it the "unbelieving world."

If Jesus brought the crowd he traveled with into your church how welcome do you think they would feel? The better question might be how long would they stay? Our time spent in church together throughout the week is meant to be a launching pad to propel us out into a skeptical, needy world. If our attendance and service produces prideful comparisons rather than humble adoration's then we should re-examine our motives.

Jesus asks us to take the log out of our own eye before we perform surgery on the speck in our brother or sisters eye. When we get off our high "holier than thou" horse, then we will see clearly and be able to actually help other Christians follow Christ in purity.

Chapter Nine

The Kingdom Has a Dictator . . . The Church Has a Committee

One of the distinctions between the Church and the Kingdom that reassures me the most is the realization that King Jesus left His Church in the hands of sinners who were supposed to organize and administrate His message while the King was absent. God set up the church with a structure of Government. This structure includes an openness to the personal opinions of the people within the church. The church is a place where you can vote or where elected or appointed elders can vote for you. The church is a place where there will always be decisions that need to be made whereas the Kingdom has a King who announces what His perfect decisions are. One of the great mysteries of the Bible is why God would choose to leave His Son's Church in the hands of men. While the Church is open for debate in deciding issues, King Jesus remains the central figure of control and He left us the Scriptures to give us the parameters for wise, Godly actions.

My uplifted view of Jesus is not diminished because mistakes that church leadership has made through the centuries. Sometimes mistakes can indicate something positive is going on. When you see the confusion and bickering in church you know things are working out just fine because men and women, all of them sinners, are still involved. There is a distinction between Jesus as a leader and the leaders of the church. Jesus is the Supreme Commander who gives the orders. Jesus is the Admiral who demands to be saluted.

This view of Jesus as a military leader was underlined for me while I was a very new missionary. Just after graduation from college, my Mom asked me to perform a funeral for a friend of hers. Close family friends, Chet and Marge Snapp had mentored our family for years. When Chet died in 1984, I took on my first funeral. Marge told me all about raising three sons with Chet and how much she missed her husband. We arranged all the details for his service.

Since Chet had served in the Korean War, the Color Guard from McChord Air Force Base was coming to present the colors to the wife of the deceased. I arrived early on a warm afternoon to a funeral home in Renton, Washington just outside of Seattle. As a final detail, I wanted to check with the Color Guard because I knew Marge was really looking forward to honoring her husband with their presence at the ceremony.

With my Bible in my hand and a song in my heart, I went to the door where the Guard was getting dressed and knocked. Initially, the Sergeant of the Guard did not want to let me in. I explained to him that we just needed to quickly go over the schedule as I slipped inside the room. No one paid the least bit of attention to me as I told the Sergeant we would like to have the Color Guard stand by the casket for the first part of the service, then present the flag to Marge. He let me know in no uncertain terms that soldiers would not be standing by any casket. The military had changed their policy and the Color Guard would simply present the flag at the end of the service. Because I knew Marge was anticipating a special time, I pleaded with the Sergeant to accommodate her request. To my surprise, he refused to give in and repeated to me what his Color Guard would be doing. The soldiers all heard this exchange and were all smiles as I left the room.

I had a smile as I left the room too because I knew something that the Sergeant did not know. I found Marge and asked her if her sons had arrived yet. All three of Chet's sons had gone into the military and two of them were in uniform that day. Tom Snapp had gone into boot camp and spent twenty years making the rank of Major. His brother, Kelly had entered the Academy several years later and was also a Major. Several years after their father's funeral both of these Majors were in charge of thousands of ground troops in Desert Storm.

Marge called her sons over and told them the minister needed them. I greeted both majors with a handshake and asked them if they would mind following me. We walked back to the room where the Color Guard was and I knocked on the door once again. As soon as the door opened I stepped in with Major Tom on my left and Major Kelly on my right. The men in the room came to immediate silence. Soldiers who were trying to pull their pants on were trying to figure out how to salute, stand at attention, and zip their flies all at once.

The Sergeant stood at attention expecting one of the majors to speak up when I let him have it with both barrels of my Bible.

"Sergeant", I said, "these are two of the sons of the deceased; their mother is very much looking forward to having the Color Guard standing at attention by the casket before they present her with the flag. Do you think there will be any problem with that?"

"Sir, no sir!" His reply was loud and clear. There was no hesitation whatsoever in his voice.

"Sergeant", I said, "I was also thinking that it would be nice to have the Color Guard stand at attention by the casket from the start of the service until everyone has left the funeral home in honor of the deceased. I know it is a little warm this afternoon but I think it would be of great comfort to the wife of the deceased, you know, the Majors' mother. Do you think that will be a problem?"

"Sir, No Sir! It would be our privilege, Sir!"

That day I decided I liked the ministry. As the two majors and I left the room, I could practically hear the soldiers exhale. I'm sure the Sergeant did not really like me, even so, he and his men had never stood so tall. They had never folded a flag so straight, and they had never stayed at attention for that long. What changed their attitude? Two superior officers showed up! It was interesting to me that Major Tom and Major Kelly did not speak a word while we were in the dressing room. Their presence was enough to completely change the attitude of the entire group.

Jesus will someday change His Church in the same way. King Jesus will return for His Church and He will take His Bride to Her Eternal Reward. If we could only see that Jesus is present in the Church today, we might not be too busy to sacrifice or too proud to pay attention. People who do not even notice the Word of God or take the time to check out a Godly message will be shocked when Jesus shows up. They will be like the soldiers in the Color Guard when the two majors appeared in their midst.

People who believe Jesus is the Supreme Commander of the Church have no doubt or hesitation in the completion of their ministry. They see a job to do and are busy doing it. They think what they are doing is a privilege. They are serving a Risen Messiah who is Lord of Lords, Major of Majors, and Admiral of Admirals.

Jesus is the authoritative distinction between His Church and His Kingdom. The Church has a central role in expanding the Kingdom. The Church is the only organization Jesus left to us. The Church was His idea just like the creation of the universe was His idea. We should be committed to the local church because Jesus asked us to and He intended it that way.

When Jesus clearly teaches an idea in Scripture, we need to be soldiers for Christ and go about the business of completing His commands without lots of whining and complaining.

The Color Guard stood at attention because a Major was present and they could pay face to face honor to their superior officer. Should we not be the same with Jesus? I know it is easy to say and hard to do, but shouldn't we be standing at attention and doing our best to sacrifice our lives for Christ? Is not being able to see Him preventing us from surrendering the portion of our lives that we are holding onto for our own selfish fleshly reasons?

Do I hold onto selfish pleasures because I have never looked into His eyes or because I have never physically been in His presence? Am I like Thomas who had to see Him with my own eyes and touch Him with my own hands? The Church has a hard time answering these concerns, but the Kingdom will have answers in full in due time.

One of the people who really impressed Jesus in the New Testament was the Roman Sergeant who understood that his men would do what he commanded and that Jesus did not need to come to his home in order for his child to be healed. Jesus commended him for his faith and encouraged the disciples to understand what had happened.

When King Jesus commands us, we should listen and do what He says. We have churches full of people who are great listeners and terrible doers. That is one reason why James, the Lord's brother, encouraged early Christians not to just hear the Word, but to do what it says (James 1:6).

The Scriptures have proved to be reliable. The evidence to support the fact that the Bible is accurate is overwhelming. The archeological evidence to support the historic reliability of the Bible is staggering. The Bible is the only book I know of that contains hundreds of name and event-specific prophecies that have already come true. Dozens of skeptics who have tried to disprove the Bible have eventually become believers. Lee Strobel's excellent book called *The Case for Christ* is a great research resource explaining how scholars view Jesus.

If every Church made the Bible their only source for structure and practice we could be confident with the decisions of the Church. Present church structure is often totally unbiblical. The fact that our buildings cost more than we give to outreach for the poor and needy of the world is a testimony to how unbiblical our structure has become. We should not abandon the Church simply because our structure and model needs to be corrected. Why not just reform the church just as other courageous leaders have done in past centuries? The facility sickness that we see in the modern church can be cured by looking at the harvest field instead of concentrating on the harvest barn.

We need a reformed church model with less emphasis on buildings and budgets and more emphasis on evangelism and the needs of people. We need thousands of equipped evangelists going door to door to present the claims of the Real Christ and not some fairy tale Mormon or Jehovah's Witness watered-down theology. We need to mobilize our paid staff and clergy by freeing up their schedules in order to give them more time to evangelize and meet people's needs one-on-one. If we became worse listeners and better doers then the pressure to deliver a message every Sunday would be taken off the shoulders of paid staff so that they could go out as Jesus commands. Jesus said "Go to all Nations" not "Wait for all Nations." We are too busy waiting for people to come to us. We are to busy waiting in the church pew for God to speak to us. Jesus sent them OUT.

Statistics show approximately 10% of Americans are Believers. That means if every Christian knocked on just nine doors we could present the claims of Christ to all of America in a weekend. The job is not overwhelming or undoable. If the church mobilized her forces, the entire world could be presented with the clear simple claims of Christ in very little time. The question is will the Church organize and mobilize or stagnate and demoralize?

Do we really need to see Jesus to believe in Jesus? No. The evidence is conclusive. Jesus is alive and He is coming back to set up His Kingdom. God will not help anyone who stands in His way. He is not coming back to pick up the church suggestion box. The day is coming when Jesus will not be interested in your opinion. When the Church age is over and the Kingdom Age is here on planet Earth, Jesus will be in complete charge. Our chance for sacrificial service to the King is now while we are in the Church Age

Jesus is not the King of Tolerance. He is not the King of Complacency. Jesus is not the King of Mediocrity. He is not the King of Self-Indulgence. Jesus is the King with all authority. Jesus is not Politically Correct; He *is* correct. His way is not only the right way, it is the *only* way. It is either His way or the highway. The highway away from Jesus heads straight to the judgment. For a further look at Heaven and Hell read the next chapter.

Honestly ask yourself, do you think a leader like Jesus is going to say "please."

Part Three

The Payment Line

The Line Between Heaven's Reward and Hell's Punishment

Chapter Ten

What You Get

The reward and punishment system laid out in the Bible has been largely overlooked by the present generation. Most Christians are happy to know that they get to go to Heaven and just leave it at that.

The Bible presents varying degrees of rewards and punishments. Jesus is the One who will decide who gets what kind of reward and who gets what kind of punishment. His decision will be just and it will be final. There will be no arbitration process. No negotiation procedure. No compromise or discussion. His reward is final and His punishment is eternal. You do not want to be on the wrong side of Jesus when He judges you. Jesus tells his followers not to judge others, but He assures them He will. Leaving judgment in God's hand is a great blessing. Who can settle accounts better: God or You?

People have trouble with Judgment and Punishment. We want to rationalize or deny, then compare our situations to the horrible sinners in prison as though crime is the same thing as sin. Skeptics say that God's system of Judgment is not fair, but there is no system that skeptics will ever say is fair. God could set up five lines and the skeptic would argue that there should be six. God has set up one line of division between the reward of Heaven and the punishment of Hell, and that line is Jesus Christ. Jesus is not waiting for your permission or consent to judge you. Recently I have realized that skeptics do not become Christians. Seekers become Christians. In most cases, a skeptic needs to go through the process of becoming a seeker before coming to Christ. The result of this realization is that I have been spending more time teaching seekers and less time battling skeptics.

Our legal system is modeled after God's legal system. Any study of God must include discussion about the Character of God revealed in Scripture. God is revealed as totally in control of every detail. He is completely fair and just because He knows all the facts. His judgments are true because He is true. The Bible warns mankind of God's Great Judgment awaiting every person. I hope you are not expecting to say much at your Judgment. Your case will be so putrid and disgusting there will be no question about your guilt.

I have been in front of a judge about 15 times. Eleven of those times, I was the defendant. I know for a fact that I never brought in a lawn chair and a six-pack of Pepsi and sat down in front of the Judge to listen to what he had to say.

When you are before a judge in the legal system, you stand. When a judge enters a courtroom, you stand. When a judge reads your verdict, you stand. When a judge sentences you to jail, you stand. When a judge gives you your release instructions, you stand. When God comes to judge every person there will be no belligerent rowdy party-ers lounging around the throne. There will be no defense attorney trying to discount and rearrange the evidence to say that you, the accused, is not a sinner.

The picture of justification in the Bible is that you can represent yourself with the prosecution team consisting of not only all the forces of evil but also all the forces of good and all their testimonies which will merely corroborate the fact that you offended God. The prosecutor will be the author of Evil and Deceit himself. Your other option is to choose to have Jesus represent you. He becomes your defense attorney and presents your case which will simply be that His Atonement paid the price for your sins. The judge, who is your defense attorney's Dad, hands down a verdict of Not Guilty and you are set free to enter into eternity with God because of what Christ did for you. At the end, the judge, knowing how evil the prosecutor is, will send all the forces of Evil to their eternal destination: Hell.

You cannot wait until after death to decide if you are going to represent yourself or if you would like the Divine Son of God to represent you. Remember, it is said that any one who represents himself before a judge, has a fool for a client.

The question of rewards centers around what part of eternity are you going to inherit. How big will your inheritance be? What position will you have in eternity? What reward will you be given for your labors of love performed out of love for the Lord of Heaven and Earth? Do you think that everyone will get the same thing? In a sense we will because we all get eternal life, but we will not all inherit the same rewards.

The Bible lists five different crowns, but you are not automatically issued these five crowns when you become a

Christian. You receive different crowns as you sacrificially serve Christ. As I said in the forward of this book, I am assuming you are interested in Bible study. If that is true, then find a concordance and look up the word Crowns. Read the passages and see for yourself if it is not true. There is a crown given to those who shepherd God's flock. There is not a crown for just being a sheep in His pasture.

God's eternal rewards are plentiful and varied. The God of variety likes different versions of the same thing. We can never really understand God. While the Bible is the revealed will of God, much of God may not yet be revealed and there is no promise in the Bible stating God will ever totally reveal Himself. We are promised that we will be with Him and that the place where we will be with Him will be better than the place where we are now. No tears, pain, worry, hunger, greed, lust, envy, pride, competition, homelessness, or selfishness, and that sounds like a good deal to me. Being with God and seeing His Glory will in and of itself be a big reward.

The Bible gives a very clear picture of our inability to understand Heaven. When speaking about the blindness of non-Christians Paul combines ideas from Isaiah to tell us "no eye has seen, no ear has heard, no mind has conceived what God has prepared for those who love Him" (I Corinthians 2:9). We cannot even imagine Heaven.

History has a way of repeating itself. Prophecy is sometimes circular, which means that one prophecy may have meaning and fulfillment in more than one generation. It may be that Heaven unfolds in the same way History does. Maybe Heaven is a continuing revelation of a God who can never be totally understood or revealed. Heaven may be a great search for truth without the guilty or envious spirit of fallen human nature. Maybe Heaven is a great mystery novel that captivates you on a perfect summer day, but this mystery never ends. Golfers want heaven to be eternal golf courses available to be played anytime they choose with greens fees paid for by Christ and every shot long and down the middle. Swimmers want Heaven to be an endless pool of perfect water. No chlorine or adverse skin effects. Every lap is at Olympic speed. Hunters want Heaven to be a safari. Some want Heaven to be a health spa with no dues. Some think Heaven will be a place where you are issued the 93% of your brain that you do not use now. Personally, I can think of people who could greatly benefit from that. Our primary and first reward is that we get to be in Heaven, whatever it actually is. The Bible talks a lot about heaven, but does not describe it in detail. What is Heaven like? No one really knows.

Jesus said He was going to prepare a place for us. He said that in His Father's house there are many dwellings, so you will probably have your own individual dwelling place. (John 14). The New Testament's mention of dwelling places is probably not our idea of dwelling places. New Testament builders often just added a room onto the existing house when families needed to expand. What kind of glorious dwelling place will you have in Heaven? Exactly the one you deserve. Keep in mind in Heaven there will be no envy; you will not think I got a bad deal and I will not think that you got a good deal. We will both recognize our rewards are perfectly tailored to our own service to the King.

After your entrance into Heaven, the next phase of reward seems to be connected to your deeds on earth, which seems odd. You cannot earn your way to Heaven, but what you do with your life will establish how much reward you get. In short, this is what the Bible teaches. Jesus said when he comes in His glory, He is going to reward every person according to their deeds or works (Matthew 16:27). The Apostle Paul teaches in I Corinthians 3 that every Christian will have his works judged by fire. Good works or properly built-works will survive the judgment of fire and each person will be rewarded according to the quality of his work.

Many Christians today are lethargic and complacent because they think entrance into Heaven is the only reward available. Proper understanding of the Biblical teaching of rewards should encourage you to start working for Christ while you still have time. No one gets paid if they do not show up for work because that's how rewards work: you get what you work for. There is no reward for dying in the best of health with your blood system filled with the latest supplements. There is no reward for reading every self-help book on the market so you can improve your self-image. There is no reward for seeking your own way, managing your own time, making the most money, or impressing the most people. There is no reward for avoiding guilt or suppressing the Holy Spirit. I have found no Scripture reference that promises a reward for church attendance.

Basically, serving yourself is not a rewardable work. Many of the books in print today start out with the premise that the author will help you help yourself. The premise of eternal rewards is in helping someone else.

Personally, I am sick of self-help books. If you are reading this book thinking it is a self-help book, please put it down and go and pray. You do not need any more self-help. You have had too much of that. Your problem is that you have not helped other people. Your self centered concern about how you feel has driven away the ability to sacrifice yourself for the benefit of someone who can never repay you. Quit reading and start helping. Go find people who are worse off than you and start giving away your life. You will never regret time spent giving, but you *will* regret the time spent getting.

King Jesus gave a partial list of what types of actions will receive a reward in Matthew 25. He also taught in the Sermon on the Mount that it is possible to store up treasures in Heaven. This is pretty exciting news for a guy like me who does not have much in the way of treasure here on this earth. We all have an account in the Kingdom of God. We can make deposits any time we want to by sacrificially giving our time, talents, and finances.

You should give now so your account is not empty when you get there. Rewards should never be our only motivation in meeting the needs of others. Our best motivation is because we love our King and want to please Him. We want to keep His commandment that we should love one another. Sacrificing yourself is not denying self love, because we should love ourselves. We should also love our neighbor as much as we love ourselves. The end result of rewards is that we will use them to bring glory to Christ. Our crowns will be thrown at His feet, and rewards will bring praise to Him. We will gladly give it all to Jesus when we see Him. Is it any wonder why past generations have put a great emphasis on holiness and helping the needy? Sacrifice here on earth does not have immediate rewards, but the dividends of storing your treasures in Heaven make investments in the stock market look like old silent home movies. Your investments in heaven will be in living color and will bring eternal returns. If you do not have any investments in Heaven yet, then get busy and start giving of yourself so your account will not be empty when you get there. One thing about money is that you cannot take it with you. If you could, I might be inclined to accumulate more money. Paul tells Timothy several things about money in 1 Timothy 6. One of the most important lessons to learn in life is that you brought nothing with you into this life and you will not be taking anything material with you when you leave (1 Timothy 6:7).

I met Michael Sawyer in 1996 and I began to witness to him about Jesus and what he meant to me. Michael asked me if I thought it was all right if he had sex with his girlfriend. When I asked him if he had ever confessed Christ as his Savior and accepted Him as Messiah, he said he had not. I asked him if he wanted to and he told me he did not want to. Based on his reply, I told this new friend of mine that it did not matter if he had sex with his girlfriend. As a matter of fact, I told him he could have sex with anyone he wanted to for all I cared because he was headed to Hell with a capital H and if he did not repent he might as well have sex with his girlfriend before he got there. I told him that in Hell he would be totally alone and in complete agony and torture.

Then on January 1st, 1998, Michael Sawyer was baptized in Horseshoe Lake along with a friend who also wants to go to heaven. They both confessed Christ just before they hit the 48 degree water.

A month or so after Mike became a Christian he gave me an analogy. He said he had been reading the Bible quite a bit and he figured that accepting Christ was allot like getting a ticket to attend a big football game in a modern stadium. The salvation ticket got you into the stadium but it did not determine where you would actually be sitting. He said it is how you live your life that will determine how close you get to the fifty yard line at the center of the playing field. Mike wanted to get as close to the middle of the field as he could because he had a new zeal and excitement to see Jesus. If this young Christian can get the picture, then what is your excuse?

Jesus laid out a system of servanthood, self-sacrifice, and death to your own desires. His system is designed to lead you closer to Him. He teaches that even the smallest act of kindness and sacrifice will be rewarded. Entrance into His Kingdom can only come from a response to accept His work done for you but closeness to the fifty yard line is purchased with your work done for Him.

In Matthew 10:40–42, Jesus lists some of the rewards available. A cup of water does not seem like much unless you have not had any water for two days. Jesus promises that He will keep track of what He owes who and that He will see to it that even this small act of kindness will get a reward.

The God of variety is also the God of detail. Jesus told His disciples that even the hairs on their heads were numbered. He taught that not one sparrow dies without God knowing about it and caring (Matthew 10:29–31). He said this to alleviate the fear and concern of men and women who had given up everything they had to follow Him. They gave up more and had fewer questions than our generation who gives up less but has more questions.

The disciples were at a point of fear because Jesus was sending them out. A major part of being a student of Jesus is to trust Him with the details. Jesus teaches about rewards to encourage and challenge his followers to give away more of their lives. His reward system is completely the opposite of the world's system. In the world, what you get or earn is what you have; in the Kingdom system, what you give away from what you could never earn is what you get.

God keeps track of rewards in books that theologians have called the Books of Merit. The Book of Life is known by most Christians from Revelation 20:11–15. When you confess Christ as Messiah your name is entered into this book. If you read closely, you will see that there are other books. These books represent the incredible detail God uses to keep track of rewards. You will be judged and rewarded according to your deeds.

Paul teaches about this system in I Corinthians 3: 10–15. I mentioned this passage earlier, if you have never studied what Paul is teaching, you should turn there now. Our works will be judged by fire. Our acts of sacrifice, or our works, which survive will be the basis upon what reward you will receive. That makes me want to give away not just a cup of water, but gallons.

Chapter Eleven

Punishment . . . The Opposite of Reward

The opposite of reward is punishment. My heart gets heavy when I study how Jesus will punish those who reject Him. The shame of having your sin revealed and burned by the fire of Judgment but still getting to go to Heaven is glorious compared to the shame of having no covering for your sin because you were too proud to accept His free gift of salvation. The Judgment of rewards is the Judgment seat of Christ. The Judgment of punishment is called the Great White Throne of Judgment.

The punishment of Hell comes in varying degrees just like the reward of Heaven. Jesus teaches that different sinners will have different punishments to look forward to. A very good friend of mine, Randy Butler, is a Pastor in Salem, Oregon. Randy pastors a growing evangelical church with over 500 members. He is a man of incredible detail, compassion, and humor. We have participated in several youth camps together and Randy always serves in the background taking care of numerous details while others like me, serve in the limelight.

Each year Randy gives a simple straight forward message about the reality of Hell. Most of the youth do not even know his name; they just call him the Hell Guy. Randy is in the process of writing a book titled *Heaven Yes—Hell No!* He has studied the Scripture for the past fifteen years on the topic of eternal punishment.

It is a very recent practice of the church to ignore Hell and emphasize Heaven. Many of the recorded revivals throughout the History of the Church can be traced to a Biblical understanding of what the Bible says about Eternal Punishment. The last great Revival in America was started by a sermon called "Sinners in the Hand of an Angry God".[4] by Jonathan Edwards.

Liberals love to avoid the topic of Hell or punishment. The New Age Movement wants to avoid the mention of guilt. Humanistic teachers avoid guilt and shame like malaria. The only time guilt is bad is if you attach guilt to some hopeless situation where you can never have restoration. God brings guilt so we will seek His forgiveness. The Forces of Evil want you to die in your guilt, never seeking forgiveness from God.

The politically correct environment our culture is endorsing tries to silence The Bible's message about guilt, sin, Judgment, punishment, accountability, and Hell. God is a God of wrath and vengeance as well as love and forgiveness.

Guilt is not bad. Guilt points you toward the fact that you have offended God by your behavior. Unresolved guilt that leads to unrepentance and refusal to accept Christ is bad.

In 1991 I was asked to represent homeless people on a television show in Seattle. The panel was made up of the mayor of the city; Tom Skerritt, an actor from Top Gun and Picket Fences; a social worker and me. We had an hour to talk about the issues of homelessness in the inner city. Within three minutes of the show's opening, I had totally alienated every one on the panel because I told the viewing audience that if they felt guilty about not helping the poor, it was because God was trying to tell them to do more to help poor people. During the first break, Tom Skerritt tried to convince me that guilt was the wrong way to motivate people to help. I gave him my 'guilt is good' speech and we did not part as friends.

The forces of evil know all about punishment. They know that God will punish men and women for eternity. The whole fight between good and evil is very simple. The fight is over who will sit on the Throne in Heaven. Satan, Lucifer, or the Devil, call him what you will, believes that he should sit on the throne and God says, "No . . . It's MY THRONE!" The angels who followed Satan into rebellion were punished (2 Peter 2–4). This was a permanent, final, and eternal punishment. The forces of evil understand eternal punishment.

Jesus teaches there are at least eleven different punishments in eternity for those who reject Him. They include torment, thirst, agony, memory, separation from good, (Luke 16:19–31) weeping, gnashing of teeth, darkness, fire or heat, being cut to pieces, and/or thrown alive into hell. These last two punishments are from Matthew 24:51 and 5:29 and refer to people who pretend to follow Jesus, but never actually commit to Him and bear fruit. The passage in Luke 12:47–48 contains an incredible revelation from God; that some in Hell will receive more lashes or stripes than others. So, there are varying degrees of punishment in Hell, and all of them go on forever. There is never a coffee break, never a union meeting, and never a vacation from the torment and lonely agony. It is Forever!

This is quite a response to the skeptic who says it's not fair for God to send the great helpers of the world to hell with child molesters. How can a God of love do that?" The Bible does not teach that he sends them to Hell together. People are sent to Hell alone.

Furthermore, they are punished differently. Not everyone will have the same punishment. God in His Divine Judgment will punish unconfessed sin and evil actions in His way. Artists from earlier centuries have depicted Hell as a place where demons torment the wicked. The skeptic will eventually find out that God is completely fair.

Many of my non-believing friends talk about hell as if it will be a big party. The Bible portrays a different picture. Hell has been described as total separation from all that is good. The Bible paints a picture much worse than that. Another popular description is that everyone is just annihilated. They cease to exist. They have no pain; they are just nothing. The Bible would disagree and is clear that in Hell people are aware of their punishment for eternity.

A simple review of the Old Testament will reveal God as a wrathful Being who is not afraid to judge and destroy individuals, cities, countries, nations and indeed the majority of the Human Race in the verifiable catastrophe of the global flood in Noah's day. Prophecy predicts such destruction and judgment will happen again. This time fire is predicted instead of water. Looking at God's track record would lead one to believe He is quite capable of punishing the people who reject Him.

The dividing line between a wonderful world of different rewards for followers of Christ and a terrible world of torments of different degrees for those who reject or ridicule Christ is the birth, death, burial, and resurrection of Jesus the Messiah. Jesus is the dividing line between God's love and God's wrath. His divine appearance is an indication of how much God is willing to do in order to show people that He cares about them. Jesus taught several parables to illustrate this point and the religious leaders of His day hated Him for His teaching (Matthew 21:33). God in His love has already waited two thousand years after interrupting history because He is loving and kind and patient. It is possible that he will wait another 2000 years, but I would not bet on it. We will look at the topic of eschatology, or End times in Part Five. After memorizing the Olivet Discourse I am still undecided about whether the present course of events actually meets end times Bible predictions.

Part Four

The Fine Line

Chapter Twelve

Jesus is the Line Between Law and Grace

There is nothing cute about God. There is nothing simple about God. God is complicated and we are not able to describe Him beyond the representations given about His attributes and His character as revealed in the Bible.

God is Sovereign. That does not just mean He has a great power or that He is in control of some things as a modern day definition of Sovereign would imply. The God described in the Bible has all Power. He is in complete control. There is no situation out of His control. God can stop or change the weather if He chooses. God created the entire universe; it was His idea.

Do you understand what an incredible claim this is? That there is a Being who created everything from His thoughts? Three key words that theologians use to describe God are: Omnipotent (all powerful), Omnipresent (all seeing), and Omniscient (all knowing).

These descriptions make up the character of God and these characteristics put God in complete control of everything.

There is nothing about God I do not like. Every quality I have ever read or studied in the Bible about the Character of God appeals to me. The fact that God gives his enemies time to repent before He crushes them seems fair to me. Thinking about God becomes a problem when we make God in our image. The fact that God never makes mistakes and yet will hold inferior beings accountable for their own mistakes seems appropriate when you see all the evidence that is available. Skeptics and liberal theologians think that God is somehow accountable to us. That's like saying you are accountable to a toothpick when you have finished cleaning your teeth. Skeptics mock the Scripture for teaching that a God of Love would express anger or wrath. "Who can believe in a God like that?" they ask.

At the top of the list of those who can believe in a God like that is Jesus Christ. Not only does Jesus teach us that God is in control, He teaches that He and the Father are one. In other words Jesus, is just like God. Jesus has the same characteristics and Divine Nature that God does. This is a not such a weird claim if you examine where Jesus came from.

My sons resemble me. They have a similar nature to mine. They are younger, but they are still human. There is nothing that will ever change the fact that we come from the same family. The same is true of Jesus. He came from God. The Christmas Story is all about an alien invasion. God invaded His planet in the flesh form of Jesus. God orchestrated these events. God left heaven and became a man. Jesus and God are from the same divine family. They are one in every aspect of personality and cooperation. The doctrine that Jesus and God are equal does not mean that they are not distinct. God was in Heaven when Jesus was on Earth. The separation that occurred at the incarnation was reunited at the resurrection yet Jesus and God remain distinct.

All of this theological talk has a purpose. Jesus is the line between the Law of God and the Grace of God. An ordinary man could never be the dividing line. For God to express Himself fully and completely, He needed to send Himself. To say that Jesus does not say please is not to say that He does not plead with us to listen. Would you expect God Almighty to ask you if He could please come in? Then neither should you expect Jesus to ask you pretty please, because God and Jesus are the same eternal, divine Being.

God's Scary Law

I was afraid of God when I first started studying the Bible. I was high on drugs one day in the back of a pick-up truck when my buddy drove by a sign that read Jesus is the Answer. I had a good laugh about that for awhile but after I got home I searched for a Bible. Although I had only been in a Church once that I remembered, I finally found a King James version from 1956 my mom had given to my oldest brother the year I was born. How it managed to get into my gear I will never know.

I had never read the Bible before and only knew that it was a book. Like any other book I started on page one. It took me 45 minutes to read three words. By this time the drugs I had taken that day had worn off and I am a good reader, but I just stared at those first three words for a long time. In The Beginning . . . What could that possibly mean? Up to that point in my life, I had claimed to be an atheist. I even made fun of Christians. My evolutionist mind told me there is no beginning; there is just now. I didn't believe man could trace back to a beginning. Yet everything had to start somewhere if it is going anywhere and certainly our world is going somewhere so where did that start? Where is the beginning? After 45 minutes, I finally agreed with the Bible. Logic demanded a beginning, what ever that is.

Then came the 4th word, and it was a big one . . . GOD. Fifteen minutes later I agreed with the Bible again and accepted the idea that somewhere in eternity past some supernatural non-human being started this entire process of time and space. Little did I know that I was also agreeing with most of the great minds who have ever walked the earth. In 1930, Albert Einstein shocked the world when he announced he had come to the conclusion that there is a God. Thomas Aquinas listed five proofs of God in the 15th century. The first proof was the proof of motion. Any motion is the result of another motion. Motion does not just happen by itself; it has a cause. The first uncaused motion is God. In other words, In the Beginning God . . .

During this time, I was working as a Longshoreman on the docks in Tacoma, Washington, and this work allowed me long hours of Bible study. On the average, I read the Bible four hours a day. I started to carry the Bible with me everywhere I went. More and more of my friends lost interest in my life as I came under the leadership of the Bible. To say that I was frightened by God would be an understatement. I was terrified by the stories of Noah, Abraham, Moses, David and the kings of God's nation of Israel. I was convinced that if I offended God, that He would send terror, pestilence, judgment or frogs in my bed. As a Bible reader, I did not even know there was a New Testament. Finally a future Bible college roommate showed me where

Jesus entered history and soon after that, I became a Christian. I was baptized shortly thereafter.

The Law of God as outlined in the Old Testament is an unforgiving system of structure. The Law was given so God would have a nation where He could send His Messiah. God was not joking around with His people. His Law is the final word. God gave His law out of Love. The Law is a substitute teacher put in place to babysit a nation until the True King shows up. Jewish people often get upset when you talk about the law like this because they think the law is more important than Jesus. Clearly, Jesus teaches that He is more important than the Law. Jesus has a respect for the Law because He wrote it, but He constantly keeps the Law in perspective.

Chapter Thirteen

JESUS AND THE LAW

Jesus is not fearful of the law; his teaching would make no sense if He were. Over and over again we see Jesus challenge the perception of the Law. His harshest words are for people who preach the law but distort and disobey it. I have taken the time to memorize Matthew 23. It is interesting that while Jesus is beyond and above the law, He still tells his followers to observe the Law. Jesus gives the impression that he does not like religion. Many of the people He spoke to in Matthew 23 were involved in the crucifixion of Christ just a few days later, so apparently, they did not part as friends. What religion has done to the Church it has also done to the Law. That is what Jesus objected to. Religion is not a friend of the Church anymore than religion is a friend of Jesus. The Law is not here to make friends with you. The law is here to tell you how far off you are from pleasing God. The Jewish Religious system added ceremonial laws to the commandments Moses received. Some of these standards were not endorsed or practiced by Jesus, for example, the washing of hands.

Jesus did not have a problem with the Law. He had a problem with what the religious leaders of Israel had done with the Law.

A perfect example is how Jesus treated the Sabbath. Throughout His ministry He heals on the Sabbath. He intentionally chooses to heal on the Sabbath to make his point that mankind was not made so God could have His Law, rather the Law was made so God could have mankind back.

It seems apparent that Jesus also healed on the Sabbath to aggravate his already aggravated opponents. A correct perception of Jesus includes a person who intentionally says and does things to tick people off and make them address his agenda. There is a big distinction between the ceremonial law and the Laws of Moses. The ceremonial laws were added through the years to expand on the commandments. The Sabbath was a target for many of the ceremonial laws. It was not only illegal to work on the Sabbath it was also illegal for your animals to work. There were additional laws for how far you could walk, how much you could cook, what you could eat, and how heavy a load your animals could carry. Jesus seemed to laugh at these ceremonial additions. He certainly did not obey them. From His healings performed on the Sabbath to His not washing his hands before eating; from eating with sinners to eating in the field, Jesus proclaimed to the leaders of the Law that he would not be caged by their dogma. Most scholars have taken the attitude Jesus expressed toward the Sabbath as a license to ignore the Sabbath. I don't think Jesus ever ignored the Sabbath, but He certainly observed it and obeyed it as a day of rest and worship.

Chapter Fourteen

Jesus Gives Birth to Grace

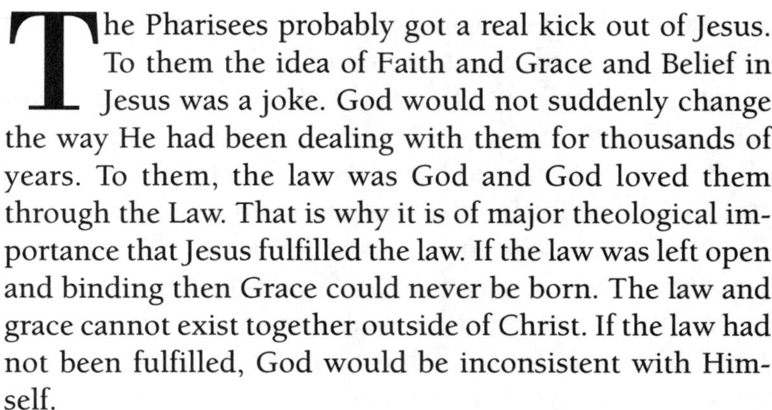

The Pharisees probably got a real kick out of Jesus. To them the idea of Faith and Grace and Belief in Jesus was a joke. God would not suddenly change the way He had been dealing with them for thousands of years. To them, the law was God and God loved them through the Law. That is why it is of major theological importance that Jesus fulfilled the law. If the law was left open and binding then Grace could never be born. The law and grace cannot exist together outside of Christ. If the law had not been fulfilled, God would be inconsistent with Himself.

That is why all of history is divided by the birth of Christ. That is why as Christians we must defend the virgin birth of Jesus with our lives. If the virgin birth is not true, then Mary is a lying whore and Jesus is a bastard. Without the virgin birth the law is not fulfilled.

There are many myths surrounding the Nativity scene we celebrate at Christmas. I have told people if they want to have a Biblically-correct manger scene, they need to throw away all the wise men and probably the animals. Knock over the shed. Get rid of the singing angels. Go out and dig a hole in your front yard and throw the replicas of the holy family into it. Find some figures of hobos or migrant workers and place them on top of the hole. Do not add any music or Christmas lights. There, now you have a Biblically-correct manger scene.

The glory of the Christmas story is that Mary had not yet had sex with Joseph. She became pregnant while she was a virgin. This virgin birth produced God's totally unique son who could fulfill the law and deliver grace. Without Him, the angels would have had nothing to proclaim to the shepherds..

When I visited the Church of the Nativity in Bethlehem I was amazed at the religion surrounding the supposed birth place of the Lord. I was traveling with a study group of students from all over the world. There were several Korean students who spoke very little English. The cave or shelter where Jesus was born has a Church built on top of it. Over the centuries pilgrims and conquerors have worn the cave down. The rocks where Jesus was delivered are smooth as glass from centuries of hands that have touched them. While we were there Arab women were in constant tears. I counted four different languages among the tour guides in the cave. I stayed down in the cave for over half an hour looking at every detail. Portions of the cave actually had bars that prohibited people from reaching in and chipping off pieces of the cave to take home with them.

Eventually some of our Korean students came down into the cave and since I had already been there for awhile and our professor had gone, I gave them the tour. First, I showed them where Jesus had been born and they touched the rocks. Then I showed them where Jesus was laid in the manger. One of them asked why there were bars behind where Jesus was laid. With a straight face I told them that was where Jesus kept His Easter Bunny.

They did not know whether to believe me or not. There was some confusion as translators told their groups what I had said. Some smiled as I winked and left to walk up the crowded steps. Santa Claus, singing angels, and the Easter Bunny have replaced the virgin birth. Christmas carols, candy canes and Wise Men on camels have become the focus of a story that changed the world because the Law of God was fulfilled and the Grace of God was introduced.

If you have never fallen down on your knees and realized how important Jesus is, now might be a good time. Jesus is not a myth anymore than the law is a joke. Jesus has been made into a myth by the same world system that made the law into a group of rules. If you miss Christ because of what religion has turned Him into, do not think that you will find a favorable audience in the spiritual world to which you can express your objections. The evidence that God sent His divine Son down to earth to explain God's system began with Abraham, continued through Moses and King David, and culminated in Jesus, then exploded with the proclamation of His students.

Unlike Religion and Jesus, the law and Jesus were friends. When Jesus introduced grace, He did not relieve us of our moral guidelines to the law. If anything, Jesus holds us to a higher standard than the law. In Matthew 7, Jesus says that the law is summed up in what we call the Golden Rule; treating others as you would have them treat you. Jesus teaches all students to go beyond the law and sacrifice yourself for others even if they would not do the same for you.

The Apostle Paul spends a great deal of time in Romans and Galatians in order to clarify the relationship between the law and grace. The bottom line is we got a good deal when Jesus fulfilled the law and offered us His grace. For Paul, the battle with the law meant that people were preaching you could not be a Christian without being circumcised. Along with this came rules about who you could eat with and how you could eat.

The real victory of evil is when the battle comes from within the Church. There is plenty of opposition to Christ outside of the Church. The Bhagavad-Gita, which is a compilation of nonsense about Hindu tribal warfare supposedly outlining salvation is in direct opposition to the message of Christ found in the Bible. The Aguarian Gospel of Jesus the Christ, written by Levi H. Dowling, is an example of another Religion in opposition to Christ. This nut has Jesus traveling all over the world before and after his resurrection teaching a bunch of mumbo jumbo about being a good person and working with the Masters. Then, of course you have the Book of Mormon, The Watch Tower, The New Age Movement, The Koran, The Life and Teachings of the Masters of the East by Baird T. Spalding in four volumes, The prophecies of Nostradamus. Add to this the Mythology of the Greek and Roman Gods, the Egyptian Worship System, the Incas, Aztecs, and American Indian Spiritists and you will find plenty of opposition to Christ.

In my research I have had to read all this nonsense and compare it to the overwhelming evidence that the Bible is historically, geographically, and archeologically correct. None of these other works even come close to standing up to the authenticity recorded in the Bible. The Book of Mormon which Mormons claimed was translated from gold tablets Joseph Smith found with special glasses so that he could read the Egyptian writing has never been verified by one single archeological discovery. Not *one*. Mormons are taught to *feel* that the book of Mormon is true.

While I am on the subject of opposition to Christ, let's not forget the incredible blasphemy that exits in the world of the occult. From the nonsense in the Church of Scientology to the Church of Satan, salvation is made into a system of following the Law of Works or following Self. Grace is in opposition to all of these systems. Grace simply says you can have God's riches at Christ's expense.

In addition to worldly opposition, we fight among ourselves. If you are a Christian, you already have enough enemies. We should unite ourselves on the essentials of the Christian Faith and let the law take its place as a reminder that we need Christ to justify us.

By the way, when this work is published, I am sure I will be attacked for speaking out in this way about some of the world's religions. Islam and Scientology have a reputation for attacking critics.

The FBI arrested a man who threatened to kill my family and me. He had escaped from a minimum security treatment center and called me from a phone booth across the street from my house. He threatened me and told me he was going to burn down my home. He was arrested several days later and served eight years in prison. People and their threats do not scare me. God is the One I fear. I do not want to have a short account with Him. If you are afraid of the Law, then you should really be afraid of the author of the Law. That would be Jesus.

Chapter Fifteen

The Line Between Parents and Children

From the title of this chapter you might think this is a seminar on parenting. Actually this is an examination into the patterns of ministry and problem solving we see Jesus employ in the Bible with an application toward being parented and being a parent.

Jesus had parents. He was parented by them until the age of thirty. Staying under the authority of his parents or parent showed a pattern or model. We all have parents. It is a universal truth for every human being. You were born because two people had sex. We all have parents, however we all did not have perfect parents. Some of us did not even have good parents. Most of the problems in our society can be traced back to parents.

In July of 1998 the popular NBC show Dateline aired a one hour investigation into the life and case of a man I know. Let's call him Jim. Jim was the first felon convicted in Washington State under the controversial 'three-strikes-and-you're-out' law. The three strikes law simply states if you are convicted of three violent felonies, you are sentenced to life in prison.

I first met Jim just after he committed his first felony. A friend at church who was working with Jim at a local hotel introduced us. Had I known all the details of his case and been a little less naive, I may have never become involved with Jim. I was told his crime was statutory rape. I found out much later that he had actually been charged with indecent liberties but was released on PR (personal recognizance) until sentencing.

Jim's story leaves a trail of shattered lives behind him. Jim was sentenced to serve time in the State Prison in Walla Walla. Just before he went to prison, he committed his life to Christ and showed growth and a thirst for fellowship and teaching. Because he had professed Christ as his personal Lord and Savior, I visited him in the State Penitentiary and arranged to have him paroled to the discipleship program at the Mission where I was serving when his sentence was up.

At first he made progress in our discipleship program. He was a serious student and he tried to help other men find truth in the Bible. Within several months he showed a legalism that began to alienate him from several people. Our cook at the time was an ex-con, ex-biker, Vietnam Vet and future Pastor who came to me with concerns about Jim's attitude and behavior.

While talking with Jim the next day, he admitted that he had been using alcohol and had been looking at pornography. I told him that he had violated our program rules and that I would need to speak to his parole officer. Jim was very repentant and seemed to understand how serious the situation was. His behavior changed and he started to get along better with other men in the program. What I did not know is that there was a time bomb ticking inside of Jim. He was plotting another crime. He was looking for another victim. Later I remembered a conversation I had with him when he first arrived at our program. He asked me what I would do in a hypothetical situation if I came home and found someone raping my wife. He said he was asking because he wanted to learn how a Christian should respond when wronged. I told him that I would call the police so that they could come and pick up the body of the rapist after I had ripped his head off. When he accused me of not having a Christian attitude, I told him I would pray for forgiveness after they hauled the body away.

Jim was looking for a victim from the time he was released from prison until the night he convinced one of our staff to take him on a tour of her apartment. She was on staff at the Skid Road Mission where we ministered. She was and is a precious servant of Christ. Her life was changed forever the night she offered to give him a ride to a local theater. He convinced her to show him where her apartment was. He convinced her to show him inside her apartment. He then brutally assaulted her for hours while he was under the influence of drugs. He committed a premeditated assault on a Christian Sister.

In what he considered was a noble effort, Jim turned himself into the police. In the resulting trial, numerous details emerged as we relived the nightmare. Jim felt that I had betrayed him because I totally supported our staff. I testified against Jim. I had his belongings handed over to our clothes room and given to the poor. I threw his keys over Deception Pass by Anacortes, Washington. The only material thing that Jim cherished, a belt buckle given to him by his Dad, was either lost or stolen. Jim was very angry with me and threatened he would "Get me one day."

I wish I could tell you that this was the end of the story and that Jim was still in prison, but Jim was eventually released and went through the same exact series of events, only this time he sexually assaulted his counselor from the sexual treatment center. Jim was a smart sexual criminal. He never actually raped his victims so the charges against him would be less severe. Jim wasn't counting on the new Three Strikes Law. One victim, two victims, three victims and good-bye Jim for life.

The Dateline NBC show was all about Jim's appeal. He is claiming that he has sixteen personalities and that the person inside of him known as Tyrone committed the crimes. Tyrone has since been killed through counseling and now Jim and the counselor who was his third victim are trying to appeal Jim's case. They believe that Jim should be released because Tyrone is gone and now Jim will never be a sexual predator again. Try selling that to his next victim.

What happened to Jim? I can tell you exactly what happened to him. His father abandoned him at an early age and he never recovered. Jim chose to ignore the pattern and model that Jesus laid out for us in His life and Ministry. Jim chose to seek self-gratification through his addictions and sexual power plays. He chose evil instead of good, and many people including Jim, have suffered for it.

Some of the pain, sin, and mistakes in your life are a result of your ignoring the pattern and model Jesus laid out for us in His relationships and ministry. You do not know about these patterns and models because you have not studied His life enough. You have not meditated and prayed enough about what His life means. You keep Jesus captured in your culture. You have let others digest the word and work of Christ for you and then you come to church on

Sunday and expect to be hand fed. You are like a baby on milk; when the bottle is empty all you know how to do is cry. I have never met a baby who knew how to fill his own bottle or change his own diaper. You cry about all the injustice you have suffered while you are covered in your own waste holding an empty bottle and accusing others. You act just like Jim only in legal ways.

If you want to understand Jesus and have Him change your physical life, you are going to have to leave the milk and chew the meat. There is no other way to maturity. There is no short cut. You have to study the life of Jesus. Maybe that is why you bought this book. You want me to do the study for you. I will get you started, but I am not about to feed you like a baby. You are going to have to invest some time alone with Christ if you want to harvest eternal rewards.

My wife and I traveled to the Salton Sea one winter. The Salton Sea is similar to the Dead Sea in Israel in that it is below sea level. I think it is the lowest place in the United States. We were guests at a place called the Fountain of Youth Spa. The average age of guests at the spa is about 70 years old. My wife and I were 25 then. We went to the pools there at the Fountain of Youth Spa for seven wonderful days. Early every morning, we would set up our chairs by the pool. By 11:00 in the morning, the pool would be hopping. We expected a bingo game to break out at any minute. Then around two o'clock in the afternoon, dozens of seniors would enter the water in the main pool armed with fly swatters. They went through a ritual that I had never seen. They would sneak around one another and then attack the water or the pool deck with a viscous swing. Then they would gently pat the side of the pool with their hand or fly swatter for about three of four minutes. Finally they would all clap and rejoice and then call out their score. This game would go on for an hour or so, then they would climb out of the pool and head for home.

This competition took place every day and it seemed that a player's score could be carried over from the previous day. By the third day I could hardly stand it. I ventured into the pool to get a closer look and started to ask questions about how I could play. They were more than happy to tell me how I could become a contestant. What you had to do was sneak up on the horse flies or dessert bombers that would come out into the dessert every afternoon. When you found one you were supposed to try and kill it with your fly swatter. Every "kill" was worth a point. But there was an interesting catch to the rules. After killing the bomber you had to take it to the side of the pool and tap the pool deck until one of the birds in the palm trees came down and ate the bomber. If the bomber wasn't eaten you got no points.

It was an exhilarating game. I did not have a fly swatter so I used my Bible. They called me the Bible Bomber Thumper. I thumped more bombers in the next four days than anyone in the history of the Fountain of Youth Spa. I loved killing bombers, feeding birds and receiving the applause of the older crowd, all in one swat.

As I reflected on our game, I realized that it was a picture of the modern day church. Dinner time arrives and the lazy birds of the congregation want the paid staff to swat away any obstacles and hand feed them their meal.

Jesus was not paid staff. He did not come to fulfill our To Do List. Jesus was never pushed around by people or told what to do by people. Have you ever really thought what a day in the ministry of Jesus must have been like? Can you imagine the demands on His time? Here is someone who could heal your sick wife, raise your dead daughter from her death bed or expel demons from your brother. He must have been constantly bombarded with requests. (pun intended) The Biblical record tells us that people were continually requesting that Jesus help them, so much that he could not even enter a city. He had to camp out in the countryside (Mark 1:45).

Yet with all of this popularity early in His ministry, Jesus was engaged personally with everyone He met. There is no record of Jesus ignoring someone who has spoken to Him. There are many occasions when people did not like the answer they received from Jesus, but He always answered. Not only does Jesus personally engage everyone with his total attention, He also answers questions with patience. Even stupid questions are given a patient response. What does this pattern tell us about how we should live, how we should parent, and how we should be parented?

Isn't it possible some of our problems as adults are a result of our stubborn refusal to let our parents be parents? Did we ever patiently answer what we considered stupid questions from our parents? Jesus was not only a perfect person, he was a perfect child.

Real revenge from God is when you have a Junior Higher of your own. God got me back with two of them. No wonder my parents left me alone after I was 13. Don't get me wrong, I love my kids and would die for them in a heart beat, but those hormones really do make a difference. When I think back on some of the grief I sent my parents through, it is a minor miracle that they even speak to me.

Jesus went through those hormone years in complete subjection to God and His parents. Scholars, skeptics, and false religions have conjectured for centuries about what Jesus did during the 'silent years' between the ages of 12 and 30. The Mormons have Him over in North America with the lost ten tribes of Israel. The Hindus have Him traversing Tibet learning from the masters. The New Agers have Him in outer space counseling the Aliens. Some Christians might think He was asleep for 18 years because they have never taken the time to learn what the Bible says about where Jesus was. It is not much of a mystery. The Scriptures teach that Jesus lived with His parents until he was thirty years old. No one knows when his earthly father Joseph died. Maybe he did not die. For all we know he outlived Jesus. We have no record of Joseph after the account of Jesus at the age of 12 when he was in the Temple.

We do have a record of what Jesus did. He stayed at home with his parents in Nazareth. Luke, the detailed historian and physician, solves any mystery when he tells us that Jesus stayed in subjection to his parents and grew up in wisdom and stature with God and men. (Luke 2:51)

The common sense interpretation of this is that Jesus stayed in Nazareth until he left on his rabbinical travels. While in Nazareth, he stayed in subjection to his parents, or parent if Joseph had already died. Most people think that Joseph died early in Jesus' life. The Bible is silent on this except for a comment in Luke and Mark where the people of Nazareth wonder how Jesus got the wisdom he was sharing. They ask "is this not Joseph's Son?" That is an interesting comment if Joseph had been dead for many years. It is possible that Joseph was still alive.

What does this pattern tell us about parenting and being parented? Our culture suggests that parenting ends when the child reaches the age of 18. Many parents step out of the picture long before this and surrender their children to the public school system. Some career-oriented parents surrender their kids to child care so that they can get back to work. Is any career worth not raising your own children? Kids easily spend more time in front of the television than they do in front of their parents. Jesus stayed at home until he was thirty.

Parenting does not stop at the age of 18. Young people need to be involved with their parents into adulthood. Recently, on Mother's Day, a prison ministry made greeting cards available to inmates at no charge. Thousands of cards were given away and the program was so popular they decided to give away Father's Day cards as well. None of the inmates wanted them. Our prisons are filled with men who did not respect, appreciate, or even know their fathers. I have often wondered if having no father figure is better than having a bad father figure. No wonder some people have a problem with the prayer 'Our Father In Heaven.'

The most well-adjusted successful people I know have or had a healthy relationship with their parents or parent. Jesus is the ultimate model for parents and children everywhere.

There are other helpful patterns in Jesus' ministry. I will give you a few more, then I hope that you will search others out for yourself in your study of His Life.

The Pattern of Information and Privacy

Jesus did not tell everyone everything He knew. As a matter of fact, Jesus never told anyone everything He knew. Jesus always answered questions with patience and He always answered questions with information, but He never answered questions with all the information that He had. Jesus was tight lipped on many occasions. He often played His hand close to His vest.

We have a structure in the modern church where the person who can ramble on about all the spiritual truth he has mastered, is thrust into leadership. There is incredible pressure on pastors and teachers to come up with new and interesting one-of-a-kind devotional thoughts to prove they are close to God. This pressure has produced sloppy interpretations and nonsensical additions to the Biblical record that are totally unnecessary. Take for instance the conjecture about when Joseph died. Who really cares? It does not make any difference. The Bible is silent about it, so why do I feel like I need to open my big mouth about it? Just because I think it, does not mean that I should say it.

Most of the truths you receive from God when you study His word will increase and mature if you keep your mouth shut and enjoy them in the privacy of your own mind for a while. Unfortunately, we can not wait to blab out our words at the first chance to impress someone with the fact that God has spoken to us.

That is not how Jesus ministered or related to people. His pattern was to answer questions with questions. He gave out small amounts of information that people could handle. He told the people he healed to keep it quiet. He sometimes spoke in riddle-like stories and always used parables to drive his points home. There is a danger in thinking that we can minister like Jesus did. We do not have all the information available to us that Jesus had available to Him. But because God has been so good to us and left us His thoughts in Scripture, we do have an incredible amount of credible, historically accurate information to keep us busy. The point in following the pattern of Jesus is to determine how to decipher and disperse that information in the best way so as to impact the listener.

Jesus had a pattern of confronting, insulting and shocking people. He confronted the rich young ruler. He insulted the religious big mouths. He often shocked his disciples with revelations or experiences (Read John's Gospel chapters 4 and 6).

In many cases, our church structure does not allow for much of this type of talk. Ministers can create more and more devotional sermons and talk about Jesus all they want as long as they do not expect anyone in the congregation to do anything they do not want to do. The congregation then agrees to continue to pay the minister as long as he feeds them without expecting them to change. If any of these two agreements stops, the feeding or the paying, then the congregation will be out looking for a new minister or the minister is looking for a new congregation.

Many churches have sacrificial staff members who lead their congregations into sacrificial service. What a great privilege it is to be involved with a Church like that.

Jesus would never put up with the first type of phony hypocritical relationship in His ministry. His pattern of giving out limited information in small dosages that demanded attention is a great model for parenting and maybe even a better model for ministry. Jesus demanded and expected change and obedience. Some of the best advice I have ever received about parenting is to choose your fights carefully and then never lose. Children need firm direction into early adulthood not increased freedom from the teenage years on.

The Popularity Pattern

After months of popularity, Jesus became very unpopular. His words struck chords of resistance from every front. As early as John 5 and Luke 4, we see leaders who want to kill Him. After He spent time being unpopular, then He went into a period of obscurity. His pattern went from:

"Hey Jesus, wow is it ever great to have you around! Can you do what ever I want you to?" to "Hey where is Jesus, that low-life scum who does not do what we say" to "Whatever happened to that Jesus guy who used to heal people?"

That was His pattern and it went on several times in His ministry. He was liked, disliked, and forgotten. If you believe that Jesus was the Divine Son of God, then you must believe that He could have chosen any type of pattern for His ministry that He wanted. He could have chosen the pattern that would have prompted responses like: "They like me! They still like me! They've always like me! Oops, for just one day they did not like me and they killed me."

He could have chosen the pattern of, "They like me and give me all their money and I get to eat honey and figs until I turn fifty and then they kill me."

There is a simple blaring truth about why Jesus chose the pattern He did. Because that is how real life is. That is how the real ministry is. Some people like you and some people don't. An old Rabbi in Seattle used to say if you thank everyone for everything you have thanked no one for anything. You certainly cannot please everyone in life and if someone has really helped you out, then be intentional and sincerely thank them.

It seems that Jesus was modeling a real person in a real life in a real world. If you want your life to be perfect and without obstacles, or if you think you somehow got a bad deal or in someway were abused beyond reason, I think you were born on the wrong planet. Life on this planet is not about *if* you will be wronged or hurt or taken advantage of, but *when* you will have things like this happen to you. What ever situation you find yourself in, it would not take you to long to find someone in a worse situation.

One of my heroes is Joni Erickson Tada. She writes her books and paints her pictures with her mouth because she was paralyzed in a diving accident when she was seventeen. One of my dreams is to someday meet her on this side of Heaven. She does not complain. She does not whine and grumble. She does not wait for someone to kill the bomber for her so she can be lazy. She eats meat from the Word.

One of my favorite Bible Stories is in John 5. When Joni was injured she used to think of that passage while she lay in her hospital bed. She dreamed of the day when Jesus would heal her. She knew He could if He wanted to. Almost thirty years later, Joni visited the Pool of Bethesda where Jesus healed the scumbag traitor of a beggar. In a testimony I heard Joni give, she said she sat by the hand rail leading down into the now empty ancient pool and thanked Jesus that He had never healed her. She said if He had healed her, she would not have as deep a personal walk with Christ. If he had healed her, she would not have influenced so many people with the message that Jesus is real. I am not sure how things turned out for the lame man in John 5. Jesus warned him in verse 14 that unless he knocked off his behavior something worse than being lame for 38 years would befall him. Remember, Jesus said this after He healed him. It is the only such warning Jesus ever gave to anyone He healed. Maybe we should be careful what we pray for and be thankful for what we have.

Jesus lived His life in certain patterns with distinct models in mind in order to teach us how to live. There is a time to turn over tables, and there is a time to cry with your friends.

There is a time to be disgusted with religion, and there is a time to allow nails to be pounded.

There is a time to leave your parents, and there is a time to be popular and wanted.

And there is a time to not eat . . . ..

The Pattern of Fasting . . .

Do You want to grow in Christ? Do You want to have clarity with God? Do you want maturity and meat from the Word? (I Corinthians 3:1–3).

Then Don't Eat.

That's pretty simple. Quit eating! Don't eat for a meal, for a day, or maybe for a week. It's called fasting and Jesus taught that after He left, His followers would fast (Matthew 9, Mark 2, Luke 5). Jesus said in Matthew 6 "whenever you Fast" not *if* you fast. Jesus fasted for forty days right after he was baptized. Obviously a fast includes drinking water.

If you have a problem that is not getting better, turn your attention toward God and try not eating for a few days. I would not recommend a forty day fast because you are not Jesus or Moses. I would highly recommend a shorter fast. I have heard all the excuses about fasting. What it comes down to is that people are not willing to sacrifice their life for Christ. Believe me when I tell you that you are not going to die healthy. You will die sick just like everyone else. If your healthy life is worth more to you than closeness to God and clarity with God, then keep eating. Please do not think there is some short cut to spiritual maturity that does not include subjecting the flesh to fasting.

We have two enemies. They are the spiritual forces of evil and our carnal fleshly nature. There is not a demon behind every tree. Some teachers have gone wacko on the topic of Spiritual Warfare just like some teachers are off the deep end when it comes to the End-Times Debate. There is not an angel or a demon around every corner. The Biblical norm is not to have angels appearing everytime you have a spiritual question. Angelic appearances are rare. When Jesus was alive on the earth, the entire planet was at an all time spiritual-awareness pinnacle. If you want spiritual victory, you should not count on angels to appear anymore than you should blame all your setbacks on demons.

Fasting, praying, studying, and serving will assist in the battle. Eating, talking, gossiping, and taking will prolong the battle. If you are always aiming the weapons of spiritual warfare at some unseen evil force you call a demon, you will miss the real target which is your carnal flesh that needs to be not only subdued and controlled, but crucified and killed.

Until you take aim at yourself and put to death the evil nature of your desires, you will not have spiritual victory or maturity. For the most part we seek our own self satisfied desires and comforts. People do not do anything that they do not want to do. Self centered carnal Christians do not seek the Lord with all their heart, soul, mind and strength. If you really do have a desire to be close and intimate with Jesus then you have to kill or crucify your own desires and what Paul calls "members of your earthly body" (NASB) or your "earthly nature" (NIV) (Colossians 3:5). Peter says sinful desires war against your soul (I Peter 2:11). Don't blame the Devil or demons for your self-induced evil and then expect to have victory. You cannot bind the forces of evil and not kill your selfish lust.

There are several weapons you can use to kill your evil nature. One of them is fasting. You will have a hard time being parented or parenting if selfishness is in control of your life. Selfishness in my opinion is the root cause of depression. Fasting can clarify and purify your outlook on life. Fasting can provide power to say no to the flesh in a way that study, memorization, meditation and prayer combined may not be able to equal. Fasting can get you off yourself and onto serving others and sacrificing your life for Christ.

The first Skid Road Mission I served in was infested with cock roaches. I came on staff in May of 1979 and some of my first training in mission work from my mentor Jack Carlson was the art of killing cock roaches. When the phone rang at the mission, you had to sweep the cock roaches away from the receiver before you answered. At first that was a hassle, but after awhile it became a cock roach killing clinic. The easiest way to kill a single cock roach is to sweep it off the counter or telephone and step on it. But the most effective way to kill roaches is to use Chemical Warfare. Sprays, bombs and sticky traps can kill thousands of roaches.

After a good bombing, the roaches would retreat for two or three weeks. Then the cock roach population would build back up and the war would resume. When we transferred and stored food to feed the poor between our mission house and the mission feeding center the roaches would come along for the ride. Soon our house was infested with roaches. One morning I got up and the roaches were having a square dance party on a sheet of brownies my wife had made. That was it for me. That was the day I decided to kill every roach I could. I cleared out the kitchen and basement and bombed for 21 days straight. The chemicals almost killed me, but it did annihilate every roach with in a three block area. Then I turned my attention to the main pod of these night crawling scavengers at the mission.

I remember coming home one night in a truck that had been donated to the mission. This truck did not have any mufflers and it was really loud to drive. As I was driving, I was debating how to best bomb the roaches at the mission and win the war. Very few times in twenty years of ministry has God impressed me with His counsel. I had a little conversation with God that night in the quietness of an unmuffled truck that went something like this:

> **God**: Hey roach killer, how is it going?
> **Me**: Great Lord, just trying to figure out how to keep your mission clean. Ya know those roaches are really disgusting.
> **God**: You know big shot, if you spent as much time killing the sin in your life that disgusts me as you do killing the roaches that disgust you, I wonder how strong a Christian you could become?

I was completely silenced by God that night. I had memorized Colossians 3 during the first months after I became a Christian, but I had totally let God down by not applying it to my life. I told God that night that I would never kill another roach. Every time I saw a roach I would identify something in my life that needed to be crucified. There is still no shortage of work that I have to complete. It seems that once I get victory in one area, another self-centered sin will join the battle. The battle will never be over, but we should never quit fighting. Fasting is joining the battle. To this day, roaches remind me of sin left alive in my life.

How are you doing with your roaches? Maybe you are a big enough idiot to think that you do not have any roaches. Maybe you are stupid enough to think that you can hide all your roaches underneath expensive clothing or counseling. Jesus asks us to pick up our cross daily and follow Him. Everyday we need to kill the roaches. If you want to follow Him, you have to lose your life.

Bad parenting is when we hand down our roaches to our children. Maybe you got a bunch of roaches handed to you. It would have been better if you had been handed a bunch of roses. Wishes do not make roaches into roses. But you can chose to kill the roaches and plant roses. You will be a better parent and a better child if you do.

The Apostle Paul outlines spiritual warfare in Ephesians 6. As students of Jesus we are told to put on the full armor of God (vs 11). Many Christians have a sword the size of a tooth pick and a shield the size of a penny because they refuse to practice what Jesus teaches. You will never receive or implement your armor through osmosis. You will not become an effective warrior for God just by hanging around mature Christians. You have to become a mature Christian yourself by applying the teachings of Christ. Fasting is just one of the ways you can grow and mature in your relationship with Jesus.

The Final Pattern . . . Death and New Life

Aren't you lucky? You get to die. The pattern of Jesus was to die. He came to die. His followers were shocked when He told them He was heading to Jerusalem to die. In the prime of life He intentionally died. He let them arrest Him. He let them put Him on trial. He let them crucify Him. You will follow this same pattern of death. You may not go willingly and you might fight death with all your strength, but you will die.

The real question is whether or not you will follow Jesus into the eternal life to come. His resurrection was the final object lesson to the world. Accepting Christ is admitting that He is the only one who knows the way out of physical death and into eternal life.

Parenting is leading people into eternal life. You are not just parenting your kids, you are parenting many kids. You are not just being parented by your parents, you are being parented by any one who leads you spiritually into eternal life.

Part Five

The Final Line

Chapter Sixteen

The Affirmation Line

People in the world often look at Christians as bleeding hearts who will help anyone, any time, any place. The mandate that Christ left his students was to help "the least of these". Refugee Centers, Skid Road Missions, and Overseas Assistance Agencies are not filled with Buddhist and Muslim volunteers because their religions teach them to leave people who are suffering or in need alone. Jesus teaches his students to help the weak and suffering. "Give to the one who asks of you, and do not turn away from the one who wants to borrow from you" (Matthew 5:42). These are the words of the greatest teacher to ever speak. Mohammed is like a child with a kindergarten degree compared to the Ph.D. Jesus has in teaching.

At first glance, it would appear Jesus is teaching us to always give and never say no. When this passage is taken in context and compared to other teachings of Jesus, a very different message emerges. Matthew 5 contains what is called the great antithesis of Jesus. The antithesis is the portion of the Sermon on the Mount where Jesus compares His teaching to the common teaching of the Jewish Rabbinical Culture. The overall public opinion in Jesus' day was that the punishment should be equal to the crime. An eye for an eye, and a tooth for a tooth is a phrase that actually comes out of a trial in Leviticus 24 where the death sentence was imposed. Both the Leviticus 24 and Matthew 5 passages are within the context of legality.

Jesus teaches that when a jerk offends you or even physically harms you, do not retaliate with abuse and threats or fist fights. Walk away. Jesus is not saying to let people hit you over and over again or not to defend yourself in a dangerous situation. Turning the other cheek means to back down and leave, concede, give up and give in. Fighting does not accomplish any good for God in a personal "one on one" situation like the one Jesus describes.

Then Jesus turns his attention to the situation where someone brings a law suit against you for damages you have committed. Jesus teaches his students to settle the law suit for more than the plaintiffs are asking. If someone is taking you to court to retrieve losses that they claim they have suffered because you were negligent, then the Godly response is to settle it. After these first two examples, Jesus brings up a subject that would personally puzzle every listener. Jesus teaches that when the government demands service that we should double our response to that demand. A Roman soldier in the first century could enlist the services of any individual in an occupied territory to carry his equipment for one mile. For Jewish people this would be especially embarrassing because of their national pride and their laws of cleanliness. Jesus says to not only fulfill the Roman Law, but to double it. For a group of students who were hoping to overthrow the Roman government, this must have been shocking news.

A cooperative response to Roman rule was dangerous. The zealots who were trying to influence Jesus would shudder at the thought of submission without rebellion. Indeed, one of the pressures that Jesus was faced with was to cooperate with the Roman establishment and overthrow Jewish input as well as the more often spoken and written about scenario where Jesus is pressured to resist Rome and restore a Jewish monarchy. In humanistic terms Jesus was crucified for not cooperating with anyone, the Romans or the Jews.

After dealing with personal offenses, legal problems and government intervention, Jesus turns his attention to social giving and teaches to give to beggars and loan money to people who may never pay you back. Jesus is not a financial counselor who will teach you how to manage your money here in this world. He is an authority on how to get a return on your investment in the world to come. Saying yes to those who ask will lead to great things in the Kingdom of God. Giving of yourself and the assets you are in control of is not a bad investment in the Kingdom economy. The world does not understand sacrifice like this because there is rarely a return or dividend on sacrifice in this lifetime. For the most part, a Christian should live a sacrificial life and say 'yes' to the many needs all around us, but we are under no obligation to always say 'yes' to every need.

For eleven years I worked on the streets of Seattle at a Skid Road Mission. I met a man there in the early 1980's named Ralph. Ralph used to walk around the streets barefoot. It did not matter to Ralph whether is was cold or wet, he never wore shoes. Ralph did not speak much either. He would wander into the mission early in the morning, stay for our devotions and coffee and then leave. I remember the first time Ralph ever returned my greetings. After I greeted him, he responded with, "nice shirt."

That was all he said and then he sat down, listened to the devotion, drank his coffee and left. The next day I put on the same shirt to see if Ralph would comment on it and to see if I could bring him out of his shell. When Ralph came in the next day I greeted him again and he said, "nice shirt." This went on for several more mornings until I finally stopped Ralph and asked him why he liked this shirt so much. He said it had nice colors. I pressed Ralph for more details, but he was not much of a talker. I offered to exchange shirts with Ralph. I told him that he could have my shirt and I would wear his shirt. Now, I want to tell you the shirt Ralph had on was nothing but a rag. He did not even wear shoes, let alone worry about his shirt. He had been wearing this shirt everyday for at least three months.

Ralph thought about my offer for a few minutes. He looked at the bright colors of my shirt, and then he agreed. Taking Ralph's ragged shirt and putting it on was one of the more gross things I have done in working with homeless people over the last twenty years.

Ralph and I began a shirt swapping relationship sometime in the middle of October. Every couple of days I would trade T-shirts with Ralph. The first trade was the worst because Ralph's original tee shirt was rank, but after the first trade I was actually looking forward to getting back one of my shirts and swapping Ralph for a different one. This went on until the day before Christmas when Ralph accepted an invitation to be a part of our recovery program. Ralph eventually got accustomed to clean clothes and shoes and within six months, he renewed his relationship with his family in Pendleton, Oregon. He moved home, got a job and recovered as much as possible. And all because he liked the colors on my tee shirt.

I remember the day I found out Ralph's real name. We had been involved in a capital campaign at the mission and Ralph kept telling me to call his dad because his dad was a millionaire and his dad would give the mission lots of money. I figured Ralph was just telling me stories to make himself feel or look important. He told me his dad's name was Woody and he gave me a number to a trucking company in Oregon. With a truckload of doubt, I called the number and the receptionist answered with, "Woodpecker Trucking." When I asked for Woody, I really thought that Ralph was setting me up. Here I was asking for Woody who supposedly was in charge of Woodpecker trucking, which would make him Woody Woodpecker.

I was surprised when the receptionist put me through and the man on the other end told me he was Woody and asked how he could help me. As it turns out, Ralph's dad really was a millionaire. He owned a very large independent trucking center in Oregon. That was the day that I found out that Ralph's real name was Eddie. We eventually received several large donations from Ralph, or Eddie's dad.

It all started with a dirty tee shirt. Jesus is the Master of taking dirty tee shirts and changing them into useful relationships. Saying 'yes' occasionally pays dividends in this world and it always produces a return in the world to come. The tee shirt trade would have been a good idea even if Ralph Eddy's dad was not a millionaire.

Even with all the relationships that Jesus works out every day and with all the goodness that can be accomplished in giving, there are still a times when giving, filled-with-faith Christians need to say NO!

Jesus talked about this in the parable of the Ten Virgins in Matthew 25. This passage is contained in what is called the Olivet Discourse. It is called the Olivet Discourse because Jesus spoke these words while He and His students were on the Mount of Olives. The Mount of Olives is actually what we in America would call three small hills. The furthest hill to the south is called the Mount of Olives. Jesus took his students to this Mount often and it was here that they asked Him the questions that led to some of the last words Jesus spoke to them before His crucifixion.

In this parable, Jesus teaches that there is a time for Christians to say NO. Jesus teaches His followers that you should not give if your spiritual eternity or well-being is at stake. In this parable, there are ten virgins. Half of them are religious idiots who do not have a relationship with the coming King or Groom. When the wise half are asked to give up the very oil that keeps them "ready" for the groom, they promptly say 'No.' Without hesitation they deny the request for assistance. It is important to note that this was a group decision. Most good decisions are made with the wise counsel of others. Jesus aggressively asks for sacrificial giving from His students, and yet He teaches in Matthew 25 that there is a time for a Christian to say No.

What does the oil in this parable represent? In both the Old and the New Testaments, sometimes oil represents the Holy Spirit. In this case, I believe the oil represents the faith and works of the virgins. The parable of the talents just after the parable of the ten virgins makes a similar comparison. The unprepared virgins had no faith and no works that would come out of a Biblical faith. There is another reason why the oil in this passage does not signify the Holy Spirit. The unwise virgins did have some oil. Jesus tells us that their lamps were burning and in the process of going out. That is not how the Holy Spirit works. When you become a Christian you receive the Holy Spirit. The Holy Spirit does not bring you to salvation and then reject you. The virgins had some oil but not enough. They were not ready for the long haul. They were interested in the short party scene and not the long all-night work party.

Is it possible that the reason the unwise virgins were unprepared was because they had never said yes to the crying needs of the poor all around them? If they had faith and met the needs of others out of the abundance of their blessings, would they have had enough of their own oil? In the context of the parable, oil was available to them had they been concerned enough to get it.

Is this the response of concerned Christians? "No, I can't help you," or "No, go get your own oil?" The result was that the virgins who pretended to be prepared missed Heaven and were informed that the door had been shut and it would not be opened. Our cultural understanding of Christianity often dictates our response to requests for assistance. We often times wonder what will people think of us if we say no, . . . rather than to ask if this is a need to which we should commit a portion of our resources. You should never give away your oil just as you should not throw pearls to pigs (Matthew 5:7).

The five pretenders made a drastic mistake when they planned to get by on the oil of others. They did not expect to hear NO when they asked. Be careful you do not get caught in the same trap.

You can not expect the faith or giving of others to substitute for your lack of faith or giving. Pretending that the faith of a family member is your faith is like thinking your presence at McDonald's makes you a hamburger. Jesus is interested in the bottom line of your walk with Him. His tally includes not only overall giving but what have you given recently. Many Christians create a fictitious picture of their giving based on a gift that was given years ago, or even gifts given by a previous generation. Your relationship with Christ needs to be current.

When Christians always say yes, it creates an unbalance in their lives. You do not need to be at the church every time the door is open. You do not need to always agree to help people even when what they are asking is important and good. Someone else's crisis does not need to be your emergency. Your family and your spiritual wellness is often more important than some of the needs Christians are meeting throughout the world. If you say yes to every need, you will soon have nothing left to give to the next more important need or to meet the important needs of your family. This is true on all levels, physically, emotionally, mentally and financially. In the ministry we call this burnout. On the other hand, if you always say no to every need because you do not want to extend yourself, you will be spiritually bankrupt when Jesus comes to claim His Kingdom.

Chapter Seventeen

The Line Between the Present and the Future

Eschatology is the study of the End-Times or Final Things. This chapter is an examination of what Jesus taught about the end of the current world system.

The writers of the New Testament believed Jesus would return in their lifetime. Apparently He is a little late. Many in our generation believe Jesus is coming back very soon to end history as we know it. The fact that one day the world will end is taught throughout the Bible. The question of *when* the world will end has not been answered.

The study of Eschatology actually begins with the triumphal entry of Jesus into Jerusalem, which begins the last week of his life. The date would be during the Passover of 30 AD. Jesus spent the last week of his life teaching in Jerusalem. His entry into the city is recorded in all four Gospels. This entrance was an attempt by the followers of Jesus to present Jesus as the new King of the Jewish Nation. The crowds responded by joining the clanging disruption in the ears of the religious idiots who were not far away from their goal to silence Jesus. The triumphal entry can be seen as the coronation rejection week. The proper conclusion to His entrance will not take place until the return of Christ to this planet, specifically to the city of Jerusalem. Jesus rejected the crown of human recognition for the cross of suffering, but one day, He will return to claim the crown. This is where the study of future events meets the dusty road from Bethany to the Temple Mount, where the Triumphal Entry of a current and future King takes place. You can find the story of the entry of Jesus toward the cross in Matthew 21, Mark 11, Luke 19, and John 12. In these passages, we have two references that indicate a multitude of disciples were following Jesus. It is important to make the distinction between the Apostles, the disciples, and the crowd in order to understand the response of the Sadducees, Pharisees, Chief Priests, and Scribes. When I first started a study on the triumphal entry and its relationship to future events, I did not know it would take me three months. I honestly did not think this event was that important until I realized the significance of this event to all the teaching Jesus does after being recognized as the Son of David or as a King of the Nation.

When Jesus accepted the ride on the donkey's colt, an event He actually orchestrated, He started a series of irreversible events. The blind and lame were healed; the children ran around screaming that Jesus was the Son of David; the religious leaders were irritated like never before; the disciples were ready for the King to take over and start the new Kingdom; and the crowds were hanging on His every word and enjoying His combative discourse with the leaders who hated Him. All the time, an evil plot to crucify King Jesus was gaining speed. Thomas Cahill in his book *Desire of the Everlasting Hills* tries to convince readers that Jesus could not have had Jewish enemies in his day[5] (page

274). You can add that pile of nonsense to the other heretical things he teaches in regard to the Apostle John. If indeed Mr. Cahill is a Christian and does go to Heaven, I would like to be privy to his conversation with the Apostle John. Although his writing is very interesting and he is a wonderful historian, he reminds me of another Thomas who had doubts about reality.

To say that Jesus had enemies and that these enemies continued to fight the Great Commission is an historical fact. Jesus still has enemies today. Jesus is used to having enemies and He may even like it that way. At least you know where your enemies stand in comparison to the fickle and ever changing crowds. On the day of triumphal entry, the crowd screamed "Hosanna!" and five days later they yelled "Crucify Him."

The partial fulfillment of the tragic events predicted just after the Triumphal Entry took place in 70 AD when Titus, a future Roman Emperor, besieges Jerusalem fulfilling the prediction by Jesus that not one stone in the temple would be left stacked upon another. While touring the Temple Entrance during my studies at Jerusalem University College, our Professor told us the story of the destruction of the Temple by Titus. Apparently the fire that destroyed the city melted the gold in the Temple and the molten gold seeped between the Herodian stones. Roman soldiers, like all soldiers, were interested in booty from the conquest and proceeded to level the Temple in pursuit of gold. The fire also produced the fulfillment of the prophecy Jesus made during His triumphant entrance into the city where His future rule and immediate death would take place.

The other events predicted during the week of triumph, primarily the return of Christ, have yet to happen. This would lead the student of Jesus to a study of these events and our theological position toward them. The study of eschatology is meant to be done by a mature Christian who has moved away from infant's milk, necessary for growth, into a more mature meat eaters diet that can withstand scrutiny and disagreement. Why would Jesus, who is headed to a cross of shame and apparent defeat, heighten the hopes and aspirations of his followers by accepting a formal entrance, a procession of triumph, if indeed he was going to let them all down just five days later?

Jesus makes reference to the fact that God was watching the entrance when he tells the leaders that if his followers stay silent then the stones would cry out (Luke 19:40). Since rocks do not usually talk, we can assume that somehow God would have made noise if the people had not. Jesus did not need to hear from God because the followers of Christ seemed to get the idea on their own. They rejoiced over all the miracles they had seen including Lazarus, the dead man who Jesus brought back to life and was now walking with them. The reason for the triumphal entry was not centered in the need for Jesus to have some validation from God. Certainly the entrance was not needed to attract another crowd of sick people to Jesus so that He could heal them even though that did happened as a result of this event (Matthew 21).

I think this event took place for two reasons. One, Jesus wanted the full attention of His true followers and the full animosity of His true enemies. Two, Jesus wanted a miniscule down payment on His future return. When I was coaching basketball in college for a small Bible College team, each year at some point during practice, I would take out a fifty dollar bill and place it by the free throw line. I would then tell the team of ten or eleven players if they could all make two free throws that they could split the $50 among themselves. As soon as that fifty dollars hit the hard wood floor, I had the undivided attention of every player. Bible college students can always use a boost in their budget and they would especially love to take it from their coach who is running their rears off at each practice. I am thrilled to tell you that no team ever took the money.

Jesus put much more than fifty dollars on the line that Monday afternoon when he entered Jerusalem on a colt. Jesus was putting His life on the line and you can be assured that the true followers of Jesus were hanging on His every word. Their attention was heightened not only because of His entrance but also because of His actions during this week leading to the cross of sorrows. One reason the triumphal entrance is important is because of what this event introduces. Just as the virgin birth is important to the Christmas Story, so the entrance of triumph is important to the passion week of Christ.

The Gospel records were divided into chapters after they were copied from scrolls. If you add the total number of chapters in the Gospels that describe and explain the ministry of Jesus you will come up with a total of 89 chapters. Of these 89 chapters, 30 of them exclusively deal with the last week of Christ's life. That means 34% of the Gospels we treasure are spent telling us about what happened to Jesus during the last week of His life. The triumphal entry introduces us to 34% of the life of Jesus that has been revealed and preserved for us to study. (this information was in sermon notes from my grandfather, R.J. Weyricks study in 1934).[6] I believe, for the last 34% of His ministry, Jesus wanted the full attention of His students and I believe the triumphal entry was what he used to teach a new perspective to them. The inner huddle around Jesus intensified during this last week on earth just as much as the opposition and enemy warfare expanded and flexed their evil muscle.

There is a second reason why I believe the Triumphal Entry is important to Jesus. I believe the Bible is a literal document. There are certainly allegories, figurative speech, idioms, analogies and other interpretive issues to deal with in the Bible, but I take Revelation 20 to be literal. I believe Jesus will rule from Jerusalem for 1000 years. I envision the Triumphal Entry as just a small down payment on this future rule. The thousand year rule of Christ is a small portion of the Glory, Honor, and Power that belong to Christ. I know readers can get bored with preaching in a book so I will move on, but I would challenge you to re-read the accounts of Jesus coming into Jerusalem or to read it for the first time if you have never given it much thought. Maybe Jesus can get more of your attention.

The Triumphal Event has two other incidents that are worthy of your study. First, the fig tree that had no figs and second, the business relocation program endorsed by Jesus. These two object lessons happen on the day following His entry into the city. I was thinking about the barren fig tree recently when I picked a sour apple from a tree and ate it. As far as I know, this tree has not been cared for in at least six years. The fruit of the tree is bad and reflects that fact that no gardener or homeowner has lifted a finger to nourish or protect the tree. The tree grows on a vacant lot adjacent to our home. The apple that I picked from the tree looked good but the taste of the bad fruit made me spit it out. I thought about Jesus that day because I had been reading and thinking about the events surrounding the triumphal entry. Jesus inspected this fig tree hoping to find a little snack. In what could be called an impatient response, Jesus curses the fig tree and the tree withers. I can hear environmentalists lamenting the poor tree.

Jesus talked several times about fruit in his ministry. In John 15 he talks about pruning vines that produce grapes. The actual word in verse two is that every branch that does not bear fruit he *lifts up*. This lifting up is a practice that is used in growing grapes in the hills around Jerusalem to this day. Jesus gives fruit a chance to grow in our lives, he nurtures and protects us so that we can become fruitful and then remain fruitful. The treatment Jesus gave that one fig tree on a very busy day was an uncommon response. I can see Him pointing his finger at the tree and saying "bad tree" much like Lieutenant Dunbar, played by Kevin Costner, did in my favorite movie *Dances with Wolves* when he scolds his horse and Two-Socks the wolf.

Jesus taught in Matthew 7 that you would know false teachers by their fruit. It is interesting that the fruit of false teachers includes preaching, spiritual warfare, and healings (vs 22). The false teachers in the 3rd millennium will continue to preach great sermons filled with doctrines that are twisted out of the Bible. They will claim to have great power over the forces of evil, then invent the forces of evil they can defeat, and claim to heal hundreds from sicknesses that return when the meeting is over. False teachers like Benny Hinn and Kenneth Copeland will be replaced by other false teachers. Fake revivals like the Toronto blessing and the Pensacola experience will be imitated and make every effort to outdo each other. There will always be barren fig trees and bad fruit. Maybe some of this frustration was going through the mind of Jesus when he stopped at the fig tree for a short break during the longest week of His life. If plotting the demise of a fig tree seems hostile, you'd better put your seat belt on because the first public decree from the New King in Jerusalem was to clear out the Temple.

The clearing of the Temple is also in all four Gospels. John records the event at the beginning of Jesus' ministry so He may have cleared the Temple twice. Matthew and Mark both tell us that Jesus was furious with the money changers and the sellers of doves. Matthew and Luke say this event occurred on the day of His entrance, whereas Mark places this event on the following day. Whatever day it was, we know Jesus is as upset as you will ever see Him until you see Him in His Revelation 19 appearance. Jesus was upset because money changers and dove sellers were ripping off pilgrims. They were fleecing the flock on a national stage in God's temple. You could bring your own dove, if you could get it past the corrupt priesthood that wanted to charge you for one of their pre-approved doves. Of course, you could not pay with your own money; you had to exchange your money for pure Temple money, so you had to get ripped off by the money changers before you could get ripped off by the dove sellers in order to be allowed to have a good experience with God. Jesus, in His attempt to protect the downtrodden and encourage the poor made yet another stand against the establishment and risked His life to clear the air for His words. When you study this man Jesus in the context of His culture you will have a hard time not wanting to risk your life for his cause. Jesus entering Jerusalem in triumph paints a picture for us of what it will be like to one day receive the King of Glory back to the refitted planet Earth.

One of my good friends is a youth pastor in Oregon City, Oregon. His name is Jon Strutz. Each summer, Jon is in charge of a dynamic youth camp called Lake Mayfield.

God has blessed this camp and through the years, hundreds of young people have made commitments to Christ because of Jon and his dedicated staff of volunteers.

One year I was preparing a message in the staff cabin when several of the cooks and counselors knocked on my door. They were afraid they would interrupt me and so they asked if they could come in. I asked them if they would mind checking my memory verses. They agreed and sat down expecting to hear a few verses. I started in Matthew 23 and continued through 24. By the time we started on Chapter 25, Jon and the rest of the staff had arrived for a planning meeting. The meeting was delayed as several of the staff began asking questions about End-Times and wanting to know when Jesus would come back to Earth.

Over and over I had to tell them that I did not know; the Bible is silent on that, and no one can be sure. Finally Jon brought our little impromptu eschatology session to a halt with a *Watch and Pray* devotion. Jon is a fifth-generation pastor and has been studying the Bible all his life. He had major questions about eschatology figured out before he graduated from High School. Jon explained to these eager camp listeners that if they wanted to sum up the message of when Jesus will return, they should just "watch and pray."

What Jesus tells us to watch for is *not* that He is coming but that there will be a multitude of false teaching and false teachers making claims about His coming. It is incredible the amount of nonsense surrounding this topic. How can an earnest student of Jesus figure out how to watch and pray with so many various interpretations from other writers? If you wanted to know what it was like to climb Mt. Everest, would you rather talk to someone who looked at a lot of pictures of a climb, someone at Base Camp, someone who actually climbed the mountain or someone who lived at the top of the mountain and came down each week to get groceries?

The preeminent position of Jesus is not up for debate.

First of all you have to put a priority on the words of Jesus. You should always give the greatest importance to what Jesus says and then compare His words to teachings in circulation. He lives at the top of the mountain and looks down on the mountain climbers. The New Age movement wants us to believe that Christianity is just a combination of all World Religions and that Jesus is just a part of the long line of Spiritual Teachers.

Peter records that Jesus is the Cornerstone the builders rejected as mentioned in Isaiah. He is also called the Capstone. There is some debate as to whether the word capstone should actually be translated cornerstone, but the two are completely different. The cornerstone is where you start your building and the capstone is where you finish your building. The Capstone would be the last stone on a pyramid, the cornerstone the first stone. From the cornerstone all the preceding stones gain their position. If the cornerstone is off then the whole building will be flawed. Jesus is the stone that the builders rejected and is now the preeminent, unflawed, cornerstone (Cornerstone and Capstone, Alpha and Omega?).

It is interesting that this same cornerstone is a stumbling stone to the religious. Jesus, as the Divine Son of God, is in a unique position to tell us when the end of History will be. He does this in what is called the Olivet Discourse. Secondly, it is incredibly useful to memorize passages before trying to teach from passages or properly understand passages.

If anyone deserved an answer to the question of when the End-Times will be, it was the disciples who followed

Jesus throughout His public ministry. In Matthew 24:3, they asked Jesus two questions. I believe that Jesus answered both questions in the order received. He answers the first question in verses 4–29 and in verse 29–51, he answers the second question (Matthew 24). This puts a very clear sign as to when the end of history will be revealed. When you see the Sun darken, you know the time is getting close.

There is a movement today to get the Gospel out to all nations so Jesus can come back. The problem with this view is that the Gospel has already been preached to the whole world. The whole world heard the Gospel in the first century. According to the Olivet Discourse, Christ can return at any time.

There is no magic in the year 2000 or 2010. If the sun is still shining in the year 2050, the followers of Jesus in that generation will look back on the hype of our generation and wonder what we could have been thinking. Y2K was hype not a Biblical sign.

I have heard people use the current fallen system of immorality as a sign that God will soon end history. Have you ever heard it said that if God does not judge our world soon then he will have to apologize to Sodom and Gomorrah? It sounds logical, but it is not true. The world was fallen before Jesus came, during Jesus' time and it will continue to be fallen until Jesus comes again. Furthermore, it could get a lot worse than this. If you say that our moral collapse will be responsible for bringing Jesus back, then you must also say that our moral success will keep Him from coming back. The return of Jesus is not wrapped up in our moral behavior.

Biblical scholars and prophecy teachers have interpreted verse 32 to mean that the emergence of the Jewish Nation will bring on the return of Christ. Clearly Jesus is referring to the Sun being darkened when he says "when you see all these things." Jesus clearly tells us in verse 27 that the sign of His coming will not be a hidden secret sign that is hard to discern. The return of Jesus is not wrapped up in the rebirth of the Jewish Nation. The 144,000 witnesses in Revelation do not need to come from a restored Jewish state. They can come from any nation. The point is they are Jewish.

The most interesting prophetic verse in the Olivet Discourse, at least in my opinion, is verse 30 in Matthew 24. What is this sign that will appear in the sky? How will the Sun be darkened yet still give some light? How will all the nations of the earth see this sign? Could it be an asteroid, or a meteor? Maybe the sun will just have a nova. Whatever it is, it will be unavoidable and final. Is the Sun already dark from the Earthquake of Revelation 6 by the time this Sign takes place? Or better yet, is the global earthquake described in Revelation 6 caused by this sign in Matthew 24?

The sun makes a recovery to burn the sore ridden followers of the Antichrist in Revelation 16. The preference settings on your computer adjust so you can modify the appearance or performance of your software screen. Inside the End-Times debate there are a few preferences or settings that can be adjusted and you can still be inside the parameters of the Biblically-correct New Testament "screen." However, if you wander outside these settings and begin tweaking or setting new standards, you will be in danger of heresy. Cult leaders are known to do exactly this in order to lead their followers to extreme actions.

It would be as if you had a pure glass of water and began adding drops of blue food coloring. How many drops can you add before you have a glass of blue water? Adding just one drop would not make a noticeable difference.

The Apostles preached the pure water Gospel, not the watered-down gospel. There are nuances inside Christianity and End-Times theories that do not equal heresy.

Chapter Eighteen

The Signs of the Times

Sometimes it is not what the Bible says that is so interesting but what the Bible does not say. We must be diligent not to add to anything the Bible says when discerning predictions and prophecies. If we examine history, are things really getting worse like the modern day media and end time prophecy teachers report?

Is Crime Worse ?

Violent Crime in the United States is actually going down while the population is going up. This does not mean that mankind is getting more moral or less sinful. It does mean that it would be hard to use increased crime as a sign that the End Times are upon us. Every generation has endured criminals at all levels to substantiate that they qualify for the End-Times status. The return of Christ is not wrapped up in the increase of Crime.

Are There More Wars ?

Armed conflicts around the world decreased in 1998 from 67 conflicts to 60. War has always been a part of World history. Utopia is a myth that was shattered by the World Wars and we are reminded daily by the conflicts around the world that our evil nature produces wars on an ongoing basis. You will have conflict using history and current events to prove that an increase in "wars and rumors of wars" is a sign that we are in the end times. Jesus directly informs us that wars are not a sign of the end (Matt. 24:6) If wars were a sign, then every generation has had enough war to qualify as the last generation. The return of Christ is not wrapped up in the increase of War.

Is the Weather Getting Worse ?

Global Warming? The Greenhouse Effect? Are there really more violent acts of Nature now than there were 5000 years ago? Is the earth in rebellion to our ecological abuse?

Weather patterns cycle in the hundreds of years. Hurricane Mitch of 1998 devastated Columbia and Hondurous. 10,000 people died and 1 million people were left homeless in Hondurous alone. This was the worst Hurricane in 200 years. The weather news wants you to think that Hurricanes are getting worse, floods are getting worse, the Ozone is leaving and the Sun will kill us. Where are the weather records from 500 years ago? Other than the flood of Noah, which is hundreds of times worse than any modern day flood, there is no substantial record that the weather is doing anything differently than it has for thousands of years. How can you possibly use the weather as a sign that Jesus is coming soon?

Scientists tell us that hurricanes are part of the system that keeps the earth's temperature at a constant level. Without hurricanes the earth would overheat, but too many hurricanes and the earth would cool down. The very hurricanes that alarmists say are a result of global warming are actually cooling the earth down. The return of Jesus is not wrapped up in the Weather.

Are Earthquakes Increasing ?

Jesus said that there would be famines and earthquakes in various places before every stone in the Temple would be thrown down. He said this would be the beginning of the birth pains. End-Times teachers have used this verse to show that Christ is coming soon because indeed earthquakes have dramatically increased in frequency and severity in the last 100 years.

Again, what records are you comparing them to? Do you have the seismology reports from when the Rocky Mountains were formed? How about the earthquake records from when the Dinosaurs became extinct? Whatever global event caused their extinction was probably fairly violent and "shaky". Are the modern day Earthquake records more severe and frequent than the incredible earthquakes that had to accompany the Volcanic Mountain ranges around the world during creation? Actually, several men have documented that earthquakes are decreasing. There could be a big catastrophic earthquake every year for the next hundred years and Jesus may still not be here. The return of Jesus is not wrapped up . . . well, I think you get the picture.

The sign that Jesus gives for his reappearance on Earth is that the Sun will be darkened; you will not be able to see the moon; the stars will fall from the sky, and the heavenly bodies, or planets will be shaken. Jesus is referring to a passage in Isaiah where God is really upset with the world. His total destruction and then reconstruction of the planet outlined in the book of Revelation has an inaugural event that correlates to the event Jesus says will trumpet his return.

Both are the same event. The sun will be darkened. That is not a very subtle sign. It's not too easy to miss. When you see the Sun go out, get ready because things are getting closer. Close, but not finished. Jesus never says in Matthew 24 that when the Sun goes out He is going to show up the next day. He says that the sign will be seen by all nations and that they, the nations, will see the Son of Man *coming*; He does not say that He will be arriving, He only says that He is on His way. You can't really blame God for taking His time with this apocalyptic appearance; it is after all, the end of the world.

The bottom line is that we do not know when Jesus will return. There are no Biblical signs that need to happen for His return to happen, so it could happen at any time. There is nothing you can do to hasten or impede His return. Jesus teaches two parables just after He informed His students about the end of the world and the destruction of the Temple. Both parables teach that we should watch and be ready for His return at any time. There are many revival teachers and prophecy watchers who say that when the great commission command to reach every nation for Christ is completed, then Christ will return in Glory.

There are several problems with that view. Two passages in the New Testament indicate that the Gospel message has already been preached around the world and that did not produce the return of Christ. Romans 1:8 tells us that the faith of the Christians in Rome had been "reported all over the world." This could refer to just the Roman World, which would still be a substantial area. Then in Colossians 1:23, Paul tells the Christians there that the "gospel which you heard has been proclaimed to every creature under heaven." That sounds like a lot of evangelism to me.

You might ask how could they possibly get the gospel around the world without the modern communications that we have? Let me remind you that everyone does not have a television, telephone, fax, or internet access; but everyone has ears, eyes, hands, feet, or some other way to see or hear or understand the Gospel. When Paul says that the message was proclaimed to every creature, I tend to believe him. If Christ did not come back to Earth at the preaching of the Apostle Paul, then what makes us think He will come back with our preaching? I am all for the Great Commission that Jesus gave every follower. I am just not ready to agree with teachers who imply that as soon as we get the Gospel out to all nations, Jesus will be coming back to set up His kingdom. The great promise of the Great Commission is that Jesus will be with His followers until the end comes.

The Thief in the Night

Jesus teaches that His coming will surprise the world just like a thief who comes in the night (Matt. 24, Rev. 16). Thieves do not announce their coming with signs of their arrival. In the same way Jesus has not used signs as a way to announce His return to Earth. His return will be sudden and global. The question remains as to when followers of Jesus will be gathered together to be with Him.

The Apostle Paul teaches about Jesus coming like a thief in the night in I Thessalonians 4 and 5. He places the gathering together of followers of Jesus who have died and followers of Jesus who are still alive very close to the sudden and global Day of the Lord in 4:17 through 5:2.

Paul also tells us that the Day of the Lord will not take followers of Jesus by surprise because we are sober and alert. He never suggests that we will have some secret Scriptural sign that will tell us when the Rapture is going to take place. Jesus teaches all His followers to watch and pray (Luke 21:36). This message is for all, not just first century Christians. This point is the main lesson in the parable of the ten virgins in Matthew 25. The final result or outcome for the Christian is not in doubt. We are never asked to watch for signs in the Scripture as related to when Jesus will return or when the Rapture will take place. We are asked to watch for deceivers or false prophets. We are asked to wait until Jesus returns and while we are waiting, we are supposed to watch out for wolves in sheep's clothing and to continue to shelter and serve other sheep or servants of Christ.

One of the most amazing End-Times passages is II Thessalonians 2:11. God will lie to the End-Times generation in order that they will be deceived and be judged. The exact opposite is true for the Christian. God will reveal His truth to those who seek Him. Christians will not be deceived by God so they will believe a lie. Therefore, Christians will not be robbed like a thief in the night if they stay alert and sober, and continue to watch and pray.

The Rapture Debate

The word Rapture, like the word Trinity, does not appear in the Bible. This absence does not mean that the concept of the Rapture is not Biblical. It is possible to describe Biblical ideas without using words from the Bible. The idea presented in the Bible and the word used to describe it is the idea that all followers of Christ will be *gathered* together with Him sometime before His Return. This gathering has been referred to as the Rapture.

Jesus talked about this gathering in the Olivet Discourse in Matt. 24:31. If Jesus is giving a straight-forward chronological answer to the questions about the Temple destruction and the End of the Age, then this gathering takes place sometime after the sun is darkened. This would correlate to sometime after Revelation 6.

When interpreting Matthew 24, you need to ask yourself whether Jesus was trying to lead his students to think on their own or was he giving them a straight-forward answer that they understood immediately? The Olivet Discourse was taught during the last week of the air-breathing life of Jesus. From other passages in Scripture, we know that during this same week the Apostles question their teacher on several occasions in an attempt to clarify what He wants them to know and do (John 14–17).

We have no such questions in the Olivet Discourse or in the parallel passage in Luke 21 other than the original two questions about when the Temple will be destroyed and what will be the sign of His coming Kingdom.

There is disagreement among students of the Bible as to when the Rapture will take place. If you believe that Jesus is Divine and that He is the highest authority in spiritual matters, then you are stuck with His teaching about the events surrounding His return.

The Book of Revelation is a confusing series of visions. Jacques Ellul in his commentary on Revelation says, "There has never been a book provoking more delirium, foolishness, and irrational movements, without any relationship to Jesus Christ as the Book of Revelation."[7]

You should not study the Book of Revelation or any other prophetic books without first saturating yourself with the words and works of Christ. Jesus is the line between the future and the past. The future will be defined and ruled by Him. The present is continuing with His permission and the future will only exist as He allows it.

Christians today are wondering if the Rapture will help them escape persecution. We can all be grateful that Jesus did not have this same attitude. If your goal in life is to never suffer for your faith, you might want to examine the historical and current suffering of Christians around the world. Why would the generation of the End-Times be any different from the previous generations of Christians in the area of persecution? Every generation of Christians, including the present one, has been persecuted and put to death for their faith. The "lamb who was slain" would not be afraid to have His followers die for their faith. Jesus tells all his students that in the world they will have tribulation (John 16:33). The resurrection proves to followers of Jesus that he has overcome the world and that we should endure persecutions and tribulations until Jesus straightens out history. This trust in Jesus to organize and implement justice is a major part of our hope and faith.

The exception to this is if God uses the Rapture as the biggest evangelistic event since the Resurrection. If millions of Christians vanish, many borderline seekers would make a commitment to Christ.

No where in the Scripture is it taught that we are going to escape persecution or tribulation. We are promised that we will not be the objects of God's wrath (Romans 5:9). Escaping God's wrath may include an early departure for Christians from planet Earth in order to avoid the seven bowls of God's wrath described in Revelation 16. Some teach that this principle would include Christians being gathered with Christ sometime before the events at the end of Revelation 6, but there are Christians in the Bible after Revelation 6. The question is, are they new Christians who make a decision after the Rapture or are they Pre-Rapture Christians? I certainly do not have all the answers to these questions nor are these questions critical to the final outcome. Christians can and do disagree on many non-essential doctrines and actually have fun in disagreeing about them. The danger comes when people start to assume or believe that God will save them from any pain or suffering because of what they have been taught about the return of Christ.

Whatever the timing involved, the events are relatively close together. The long struggle will someday be over and the winning side will be those who have chosen to stand behind Jesus. If you have Jesus, you own more than a winning lottery ticket. If you have Jesus, you do not need to wait for the next Publishers Clearing House drawing because you have already won. The Christian is never offered a free pass through the emotional and physical difficulties of life. Jesus may even allow you to have more problems and barricades when He is given control of your life. The promise Jesus gives is that in the end He will conquer death.

I remember explaining these ideas to a convict who had just been released from Prison. He was unemployed and living in one of the low income rooms in the mission where I served. His name was Jim Banks but everyone just called him JB.

I first met JB in a parking lot near Skid Road in Seattle. He looked like he had just climbed off a Harley Davidson Motorcycle. JB had tattoos down both his shoulders that he had given to himself when he was in the Federal Penitentiary. He was a stocky Neanderthal-looking man in his late thirties. I asked him if he would be interested in attending a Bible study and to my surprise he accepted. Later that same night, I invited him to come into the mission discipleship program and again to my surprise he accepted. I studied the Bible with JB for over three years. He eventually became the cook in the mission and discipled others.

JB had a hard time transitioning into the Christian world. He had lied about his age and entered the military at the age of 17, then served in Viet Nam. After returning from Southeast Asia, he spent 11 years in a motorcycle gang in West Seattle before he was sentenced to four years in prison.

God used his unconventional life to reach dozens of people for Christ. JB enrolled in a Bible college and eventually became a youth minister in Oroville, California. When the preaching minister resigned, JB took over the Pulpit.

The church secretary was in her office one day when a strange man came into the building and knocked on her door. She had a weird feeling about the man and his appearance so she locked her door and called JB in his office at the other end of the church. By the time JB arrived at the secretary's office, the man was knocking on the door with a knife.

JB turned him around and punched him square in the nose without saying a word. The man staggered to the floor and JB told the secretary to call 911. Then the intruder stood and charged at JB with the Knife. JB hit him so hard he knocked him through the sanctuary doors and under one of the Church pews. The police arrived and put JB in hand cuffs and were in the process of leading him to the police car when the church secretary finally convinced them that JB was the Pastor and the guy who was passed out under the Church pew was the one who was trying to assault her. Later, the police called and told JB that the man was an escapee from jail and there were outstanding warrants for his arrest. I guess God knew which church to let a renegade outlaw go to in the Oroville area.

When our two boys were younger, we occasionally asked JB to babysit. One night we went out to dinner and left JB in charge. Early in the evening, my mother in-law dropped by to say hello and was shocked to see that we had left our sons with someone "from the mission who looked like a freaked-out drug addict." She called after we returned home and asked me if I thought it was safe to leave the kids with JB. I assured her that they were as safe with JB as they were with me, maybe safer.

I wish I could tell you that JB was still a minister in Oroville. Within two years of his ordination and marriage, he contracted a form of cancer in his blood. He died of a blood clot in his heart. In the long run everything did work out for JB. He was on the winning side of the only fight that will really matter in eternity.

Christianity is not a promise that everything will go well. Christianity is a promise that everything well end up well. Wise Virgins keep this in mind when considering future predictions about coming End Times events. However these events unfold, I am looking forward to seeing JB someday. That is one of the promises in the Gospel.

We tend to hide behind what we do for a living as if this defines who we are. That was the interesting thing about Jesus, he quickly got through the outer issues in his relationships with people and confronted them with the problems that really mattered. He still does this today in the Church.

A suit can be like a uniform you wear when you show up for work. You become official when you put it on. What you do for a living can become something similar in your relationship to God. Your occupation can become a shield that keeps God away from the real you. For me, serving homeless families can be a front so that other Christians think highly of me for being a slave to God, when in fact service can become a thick shield to keep God away from confronting the real problems that He would like me to address. Jesus died to get your attention. Nothing is hidden from God's sight. Everything is laid bare before the eyes of Him to whom we must give account (Hebrews 4).

Compared to the Human mind, bugs and insects are intellectual midgets. Grasshoppers do not recite poetry, mosquitoes do not play musical instruments, and flies and bees cannot talk. Compared to the Divine mind, the human mind is like a bug. We can not see into the future any more than a bug can understand calculus. Our minds are limited. The information in Scripture is limited. And so our understanding of Eschatological events is limited.

The summation of what the Bible teaches is that we do not know when the end of history will come, yet there will be unmistakable signs of its coming. Jesus wins in the end and until then we should watch and pray, not guess and predict.

A Word about False Prophets

Spiritual frauds and advisors peddle significance to the affluent or the needy. The psychic line with a toll free number will tell you how the universe revolves around you. Not only are the church and secular world preyed upon by cults and idol worship, false prophets inside the church deceive well-intentioned followers with blatant lies and fabrications. They try to convince people how important they are while offering trinkets and prayer cloths. Religious tolerance has invaded the Church just like political tolerance has set up shop in Washington DC. The close election in the year 2000 was nothing new. The real question is whether or not our constitution will survive the onslaught of liberalism.

God does look upon mankind as redeemable and worthy of His attention. The whole point of worship is that God is infinitely more important than we are. False teachers typically view themselves as equal to God. They act as if they are doing God a favor by acknowledging Him. If you are so significant and important, then change the way the wind is blowing instead of blowing so much hot air. Your swollen impression of yourself distorts God's call in your life. Your puffed up pride has produced a barrier that offends Jesus. Your openness to your own truth has shielded you from His truth. While you persist in your aggression and continue to water down the Gospel with liberalism, prosperity, significance, and pride, you should know this: Jesus *will* hold you accountable.

Picture a small ant scampering back and forth on the pavement. This little ant can carry over thirty times it's own weight upside down. Pretty significant accomplishment! Then picture the heel of your shoe crushing the ant into dust. False Prophets and the entire world of evil is like an ant under the coming thunderous feet of Jesus.

In the Bible, false prophets usually assured leadership that they had no flaws. False prophets continually built up the significance and importance of the affluent and successful. When Isaiah, Jeremiah, Daniel, Ezekiel, or Amos spoke about God's mighty hand of Judgment against the affluent economy or the idolatrous leadership they were threatened with ridicule, imprisonment and execution.

Today's modern intellectual and minimalist teachers are slowly repeating this process. Orthodox doctrines like the virgin birth of Christ and the Resurrection are berated, belittled, and pushed aside. People who stand up for God are ridiculed in the media as fanatics. Communicating God's truth and control while presenting mankind's individual insignificance in time and space is considered heretical.

The false prophets of the prosperity gospel and the false prophets of the Jesus Seminar[8] both preach about individual significance as if what happens to you in this life is the most important concern. Jesus taught that this life will give way to another life that is eternal. His promise is that He will be in charge of not only this life but also of the life to come. True Biblical insignificance comes out of a humble heart. When Jesus taught about cutting off your hand or foot, and plucking out your eye, He was teaching about the insignificance of the air-breathing individual in comparison to the eternal world beyond this life. He is not asking you to dismember your body, rather He is asking you to build up your spirit through humility.

The economics of humility will cost you time and money. King David refused the gift of Araunah in I Chronicles 20 saying "I refuse to make an offering that cost me nothing." David was humbled by God after the pride of a census brought on a plague that killed 70,000 of his men. We all need to pass through the fires of humility. Seeing yourself as insignificant in comparison to God is actually a comfort. The humble insignificant can wait for God to answer whereas the mighty significant have to conquer every problem. Being insignificant in the grand scheme of the universe does not mean that life is meaningless or hopeless. Being insignificant does not relieve you of the personal responsibility of God's call on your life. God raises up the insignificant to mighty works in partnership with Him and yet demands that they remain humble, giving significance to God alone. That is, after all, what God deserves.

ENDNOTES

1. Yancey, Philip. *The Jesus I Never Knew* (Zondervan: 1995), pages 49–65.

2. Max Lucado was a speaker when I attended the Pastors Conference in Atlanta. These are my recollections from a sermon by Max Lucado at the Promise Keepers Conference in Atlanta. As far as I know these comment have not been published.

3. I am not sure what the title of this old hymn is. I bet if you asked an older saint about this hymn they would know the name. This is one of my points about spiritual rewards. Past generations understood the Biblical teaching and importance of working for Christ. The old hymns of the Church are a great teaching tool in many cases and should not be replaced with silly songs about how we feel.

4. Jonathan Edwards was a revival preacher and pastor. His work has recently been rediscovered by younger Christians. The sermon mentioned is credited with awakening America to the reality of punishment. You may be able to obtain a copy of this sermon from the writings of Jonathan Edwards at a local Christian Book Store.

5. Cahill, Thomas. *The Desire of the Everlasting Hills.* (Doubleday: 1999) page 274.

6. My Grandfather was a minister for over fifty years. When he went to Heaven I inherited his study notes. I wanted to give him credit for the research.

7. This was in a Christian Leadership Magazine from 1999.

8. The Jesus Seminar is a group of liberal scholars who have decided that much of what Jesus said is not historically accurate. They have received publicity on the front cover of Time Magazine as well as many Newspapers. When you see a documentary that denies Jesus is divine or that He was resurrected from the dead, chances are the scholar they show will know all about the Jesus Seminar.